The Protractor Handbook

Understanding and Implementing the Tool Effectively

Shashank Shukla

Apress®

The Protractor Handbook: Understanding and Implementing the Tool Effectively

Shashank Shukla
Mandla, Madhya Pradesh, India

ISBN-13 (pbk): 978-1-4842-7288-6   ISBN-13 (electronic): 978-1-4842-7289-3
https://doi.org/10.1007/978-1-4842-7289-3

Managing Director, Apress Media LLC: Welmoed Spahr
Acquisitions Editor: Shiva Ramachandran
Development Editor: Matthew Moodie
Coordinating Editor: Jessica Vakili

Distributed to the book trade worldwide by Springer Science+Business Media New York, 1 New York Plaza, New York, NY 100043. Phone 1-800-SPRINGER, fax (201) 348-4505, e-mail orders-ny@springer-sbm.com, or visit www.springeronline.com. Apress Media, LLC is a California LLC and the sole member (owner) is Springer Science + Business Media Finance Inc (SSBM Finance Inc). SSBM Finance Inc is a **Delaware** corporation.

For information on translations, please e-mail booktranslations@springernature.com; for reprint, paperback, or audio rights, please e-mail bookpermissions@springernature.com.

Apress titles may be purchased in bulk for academic, corporate, or promotional use. eBook versions and licenses are also available for most titles. For more information, reference our Print and eBook Bulk Sales web page at http://www.apress.com/bulk-sales.

Any source code or other supplementary material referenced by the author in this book is available to readers on GitHub via the book's product page, located at www.apress.com/9781484272886. For more detailed information, please visit http://www.apress.com/source-code.

Printed on acid-free paper

This book is dedicated to my loving wife, Anuja, and my son, Riyaarth, for consistently providing me an incredible support system to thrive on.

Table of Contents

About the Author

Shashank Shukla has been working in software testing for more than a decade. He is passionate about tools and technology that can be leveraged to enrich the testing experience and optimize the quality of delivery.

About the Technical Reviewer

Rami Morrar is a self-taught programmer and has coding experience in languages such as C# and C++. His projects include a gaming tutorial website, several desktop applications, and games in the Unity game engine. He is currently working on his own independent game project in the MonoGame framework, set to be released next year. Rami is passionate about programming and game development and is co-writing the second edition of the book *MonoGame Mastery* (first edition, Apress, 2020). In his free time, he likes to play games and look at cool new projects by other indie developers.

Acknowledgments

Many thanks to the generous people of the open source community who contribute each day selflessly to make modern test automation tools easy to use and help people implement smarter testing approaches.

I'd like to thank everyone at Apress who helped make this book possible and put up with the fumbling efforts of a novice author.

I would also like to thank my employer Azuga Inc., my engineering manager, Sindhoora Ramesh, test manager, Rohit Naarayanan, and colleagues, Shubham Sharma & Logesh Kumar, for providing a conducive and healthy work environment of mentorship and support. Also, I have not forgotten the software testers and consultants I have worked with so far and learned from throughout my career. Without your help, this book would not have been written!

And finally, I want to thank my mom, dad, and wife, who tirelessly managed everything else, giving me the luxury of time needed while I completed this book over the last year.

CHAPTER 1

Getting Started

Browser automation is evolving by leaps and bounds. The cornerstones of this transformation are the new frameworks based on Node.js that are being released. JavaScript had already dominated front-end development since its genesis. Now, with frameworks for languages such as Node.js with its server-side capabilities, it is making its presence known in back-end development. Due to the recent domination of JavaScript in front-end and back-end development, many test automation architects make design decisions that utilize Node.js-based automation frameworks to leverage features like ease of use, application compatibility, and resource cross-utilization.

Angular is the most popular front-end framework for creating dynamic and single-page applications and web pages. It is an open source framework maintained by Google. Figure 1-1 shows the top-ten web sites running on Angular.

© Shashank Shukla 2021
S. Shukla, *The Protractor Handbook*, https://doi.org/10.1007/978-1-4842-7289-3_1

Top Websites Using Angular JS		
▸ youtube.com	**2** TRAFFIC RANK	**34.2B** MONTHLY VISITS
▸ m.youtube.com		**5.7B** MONTHLY VISITS
Y! news.yahoo.co.jp	**42** TRAFFIC RANK	**953.5M** MONTHLY VISITS
G doubleclick.net		**912.3M** MONTHLY VISITS
G google.com.br	**27** TRAFFIC RANK	**877.8M** MONTHLY VISITS
▸ translate.google.com		**775M** MONTHLY VISITS
▪ roblox.com	**36** TRAFFIC RANK	**609.9M** MONTHLY VISITS
G google.de	**45** TRAFFIC RANK	**573M** MONTHLY VISITS
▪ web.roblox.com		**386.3M** MONTHLY VISITS
G google.co.jp	**59** TRAFFIC RANK	**380.6M** MONTHLY VISITS

Figure 1-1. *Top 10 web sites built on Angular (Source: SimilarTech)*

Protractor is a Node.js-based automation framework, also developed by Google. It is a go-to choice for testing Angular applications because Google customizes it to work well with Angular components that spawn in the DOM of the web page.

This chapter briefly introduces Protractor. You will also learn how to install Protractor and swiftly get to a point where you can run your first test. The chapter covers the following.

- What Protractor is

- Why Protractor is gaining popularity among the new generation of test engineers

- How to install Protractor

- How to run your first test in minutes

- Additional steps to take in case the installation fails

- Demo web sites to practice test automation

Introduction

Protractor is a customized implementation of the official Selenium API, which is based on JavaScript and packaged as `selenium-webdriver` under the npm package, which runs on Node.js. Protractor abstracts all the lengthy syntax and complex asynchronous promise management of underlying JavaScript and presents users with easy-to-read-and-remember action commands. It makes every test step synchronous, meaning the user doesn't have to worry about any missed steps in the test code. The framework is flexible; however, it comes with *Jasmine* as its test framework by default.

It is packaged and installed through npm and runs on Node.js, which is a JavaScript runtime environment that allows you to run JavaScript outside of your browser. It can run on macOS, Linux, and Windows.

The principal reason it is thriving in the marketplace is due to its matured implementation of the Selenium API to tackle Angular-specific components and timeouts. Anyone experienced in working with other JavaScript frameworks can get started with this tool in no time. Figure 1-2 depicts the growing popularity of this tool. The Protractor framework was downloaded almost 1.4 million times during one week in 2021.

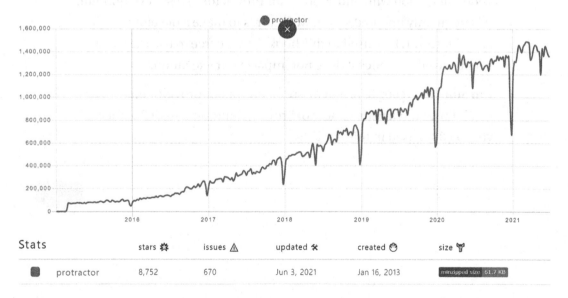

Figure 1-2. *Growing popularity of Protractor (Source: `www.npmtrends.com`)*

Installation

The Protractor installation process is very easy. This book explains the step-by-step process of installing it on Windows 10. You need an active Internet connection and enough space on your machine to accommodate the setup.

Prerequisites

The following covers the basic tools required for a bare-bones Protractor project setup.

- **Node.js** (`https://nodejs.org/en/download/`). Download the LTS (latest stable version) or the current version with the latest features. If you are using Node.js for the first time, it downloads in the default location suggested by your operating system, which applies to all the recommended tools in this book. Node.js version 14.15.5 (`https://nodejs.org/en/blog/release/v14.15.5/`) is used in this book. I recommend you use the latest version if it's not compatible with Chrome (or any other browser) to avoid any errors that crop up due to version mismatch.

- **Visual Studio Code** (`https://code.visualstudio.com/download`) is a widely used free code editor in the JavaScript universe. It provides good integration with and support for Protractor in test development. It is frequently updated with new features to make a developer's life easy. Version 1.49 is used in this book. You are free to use the latest version available since it does not impact your execution.

- **Chrome** (`www.google.com/chrome/`). Protractor provides the flexibility to test a wide variety of browsers and versions. Chrome version 88 is used in this book.

> **Note**   If you are using the latest version of Node.js, you might need to install
> Python (`https://docs.python.org/3/using/`) or JDK (`https://`
> `docs.oracle.com/en/java/javase/11/install/overview-jdk-`
> `installation.html`). Do this only if there is an error that says, "Can't find
> Python executable "python", you can set the PYTHON env variable," which
> specifically asks you to install Python. For more information on why Node.js needs
> Python, refer to `https://stackoverflow.com/questions/23709739/why-`
> `does-node-js-need-python`.

Installation Process

Once you get these applications installed, create a folder named Protractor and open it via Visual Studio Code by right-clicking "Open with Code" (see Figure 1-3).

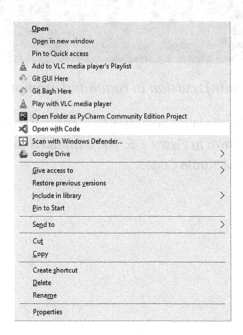

Figure 1-3. *Visual Studio Code options when right-clicked*

At the same time, you can check the Node.js installation and version by opening your command prompt and typing **node -v**, as shown in Figure 1-4. This confirms that Node.js is installed in your system.

Figure 1-4. *Checking Node.js version in command prompt*

Once Visual Studio Code is launched, click the Terminal option in the menu bar and select New Terminal, as shown in Figure 1-5. The terminal is the Windows command prompt embedded in Visual Studio Code.

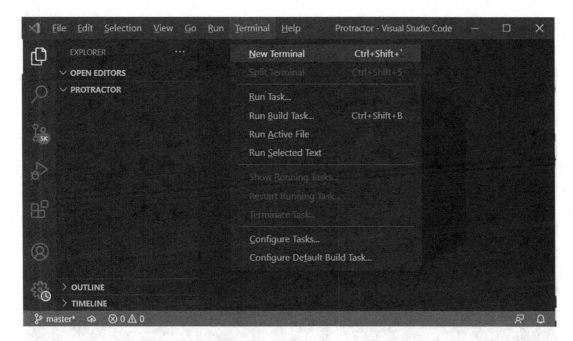

Figure 1-5. *Visual Studio New Terminal option*

In the newly opened terminal, type the following command to initiate a node project. It creates a `package.json` file to manage all your project dependencies (see Figure 1-6).

```
npm init -y
```

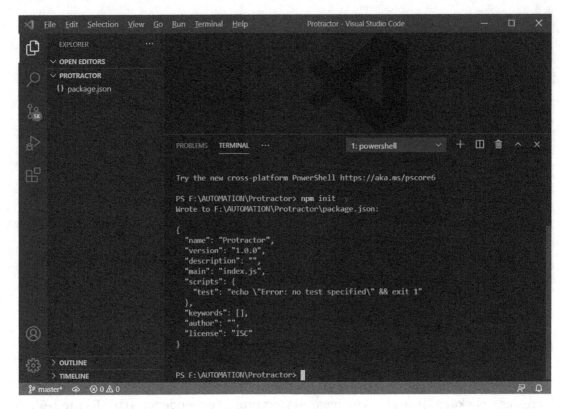

Figure 1-6. *Default Package.json file looks like this*

Next, enter the following command, which installs Protractor on your local machine.

```
npm install protractor@7.0.0 --save-dev
```

To elaborate on what this command does, you need to understand what npm is. The Node Package Manager can be compared to Google Playstore. You can download any app from Playstore. Similarly, from npm, you can get any package developed and published by any Node.js programmer around the world and include it as part of your Node.js application. In the command, you call the Protractor package via npm. The @ specifies that you need the 7.0.0 version of this package. The --save-dev options specify that you need it to be saved to the local repository as a dev dependency (see Figure 1-7). If you want access across any project on your Windows machine, use –g instead of the --save-dev parameter and install it globally. The Protractor package comprises other components, which you see shortly.

Figure 1-7. *Protractor installation successful*

When you open package.json, you see the Protractor library in devDependencies, as shown in Figure 1-8.

Figure 1-8. *package.json file*

However, there are a lot of other packages that Protractor depends on (see Figure 1-9), which have also been installed and can be found inside the node_modules folder. *Jasmine* is the default test framework and Selenium WebDriver runs the test cases.

protractor

7.0.0 • Public • Published 9 months ago

| 📄 Readme | 📘 Explore BETA | 🎁 15 Dependencies | 🥨 |

Dependencies (15)

@types/q @types/selenium-webdriver blocking-proxy browserstack chalk glob

jasmine jasminewd2 q saucelabs selenium-webdriver source-map-support

webdriver-js-extender webdriver-manager yargs

Dev Dependencies (28)

@types/chalk @types/glob @types/jasmine @types/jasminewd2

@types/minimatch @types/node @types/yargs body-parser chai

chai-as-promised clang-format expect.js express gulp gulp-clang-format

gulp-tslint jshint lodash marked mocha natives rimraf run-sequence semver

tslint tslint-eslint-rules typescript vrsource-tslint-rules

Figure 1-9. *Dev dependencies of protractor package*

Let's quickly make some basic project structures to organize the test cases. Create a test folder and a file named spec.js inside it. Also, create a pageobjects folder, which is used in the later chapters of this book. In the spec.js file, add the code provided in Listing 1-1.

Listing 1-1. Sample Code for the spec.js File

```
describe('Protractor Demo App', function () {
    it('should have a title', function () {
        browser.get('http://juliemr.github.io/protractor-demo/');
        expect(browser.getTitle()).toEqual('Super Calculator');
    });
});
```

For now, let's focus on the describe and it keywords. These keywords come from the Jasmine framework.

Protractor is an end-to-end automation framework. End-to-end (or E2E) testing tests whether the flow of an application is behaving as expected from the first to the final steps. The Protractor automation framework lets you develop E2E test scripts with support from the behavior-driven development (BDD) framework (Jasmine, Mocha, or Cucumber), which is required for structuring these test scripts. Jasmine, which is classified as a behavior-driven framework, primarily *organizes* your test cases neatly for you to read, so you don't have to go through random lines of code to figure out where a test case starts and where it ends. For more information, visit https://jasmine.github.io/.

describe creates a suite of test cases, and with the help of it blocks, you implement individual test cases within the suit. The first argument in an it block describes the test case, and the next argument is a JavaScript arrow function (()=>). The arrow function is used for the simplicity of its syntax in Mocha. The functions in it and describe blocks are anonymous. There can be multiple it blocks inside one describe block. You can have nested describe blocks, but you shouldn't nest it blocks because it might cause issues while running the test cases.

The folder is created because you are looking at the Page Object Model (POM) design pattern to manage test scripts in this framework. The purpose of the Page Object Model is to completely encapsulate a web page's testing interface in one place, which can be a .js file, so that the tester understands that if the change is made on a specific page on the web site, which part of the automation suite consequently requires corresponding changes. The Page Object Model also abstracts all the irrelevant information from the actual tests so that your test cases are legible and unnecessary details like locators, test data, and functions are hidden from the tester in day-to-day execution. The focus of this book is to make you aware of all the API methods available in Protractor so you can easily automate the user's interactions with the web page. Hence you delve into page objects after all the APIs provided by Protractor have been covered.

Create a conf.js file at the root of your project directory and copy the contents from Listing 1-2.

Listing 1-2. Sample Config File

```
exports.config = {
    framework: 'jasmine',
    seleniumAddress: 'http://localhost:4444/wd/hub',
    specs: ['test/spec.js']
}
```

At this moment, your framework should look as per Figure 1-10.

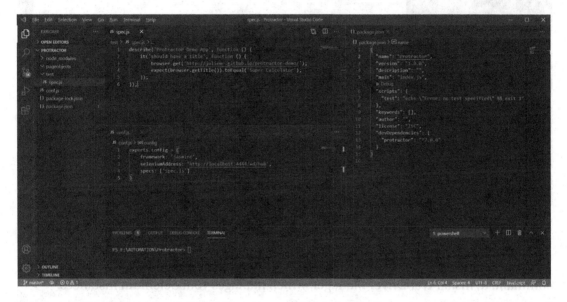

Figure 1-10. *Framework folder structure with a tabbed view of spec.js, conf.js, and package.json*

If you are installing Protractor locally instead of globally, make sure that your environment variable is set up to point to the `.bin` folder located inside `node_modules` in your project folder, as shown in Figure 1-11. Installing the npm packages locally is always a good practice because it allows you to run different versions of Protractor in the same machine, as all projects have their own local version of the Protractor package. You can check if you have any packages installed globally using `npm list -g --depth 0` to avoid conflict.

13

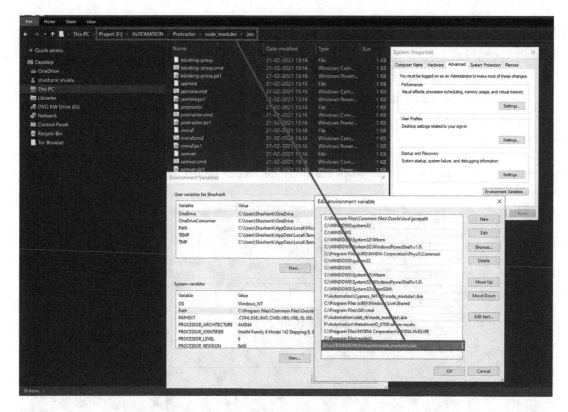

Figure 1-11. *Setting up the environment variable*

After setting up the environment and restarting Visual Studio Code, run the following command to install WebDriver Manager, which manages your Selenium instances.

```
webdriver-manager update
```

Type the following command to start the Selenium session that acts as a bridge between your test scripts and browser.

```
webdriver-manager start
```

You should see the Selenium server up and running confirmation on your log, as highlighted in Figure 1-12. Make sure that you do this in case you get the following error, which means that the Selenium server is currently stopped.

```
"ECONNREFUSED connect ECONNREFUSED 127.0.0.1:4444"
```

Figure 1-12. *Selenium WebDriver launched by webdriver-manager package*

Open a new terminal by pressing the + (plus sign), highlighted in green in Figure 1-12, and fire the following command. This initiates your spec execution.

```
protractor conf.js
```

Finally, you see the browser spinning up and closing down on your machine. Congrats! You have a bare-bones Protractor framework ready.

A green dot represents the number of specs in the generated log and its status. Figure 1-13 shows one passed spec that finished in 28 seconds. You see more evolved reports in upcoming chapters.

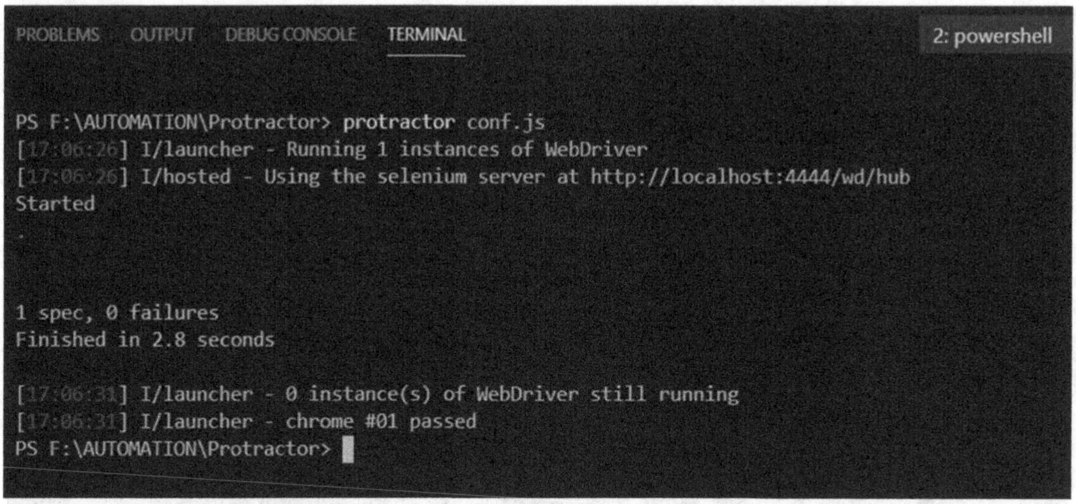

Figure 1-13. *Console logs after a successful run*

The test launches the default browser, navigates to `http://juliemr.github.io/protractor-demo/`, and verifies if the title of the web page displayed in the title bar is Super Calculator. If the execution was too fast, you can manually visit the web page and verify the title with the provided expected result shown in Listing 1-1. I urge you to change the expected result in the code deliberately and observe the test case failing. Please note that the browser automatically shuts down once the execution is complete, irrespective of the test case passing or failing. What other things can you find in the terminal after running the spec file?

Additional Information

Version mismatch can be a real pain in Node.js/JavaScript-based frameworks, so if you are still unable to run the test script after following the installation steps, be sure to reinstall the latest stable versions of Chrome, Node.js, and Protractor.

Summary

This chapter introduced Protractor, its prerequisites, and installation process.

In the next chapter, you learn about locators and how Protractor's highly customized locator strategies uniquely identify Angular elements.

The following are some of the demo web sites used throughout the book for coded demonstrations.

- Angular

    - `http://juliemr.github.io/protractor-demo/`

    - `www.protractortest.org`

    - `https://angular.realworld.io/`

- Non-Angular

    - `https://the-internet.herokuapp.com`

CHAPTER 2

Selenium-Inherited Web Locators

Now that your framework is installed and your first test case is running successfully, let's proceed to the next step. This chapter explains how to locate the elements of a web page so that they can be interacted with. You will also learn about different locator strategies that Protractor inherits from Selenium WebDriver (`webdriver.By`) library, including the following.

- Taking a screenshot of an identified locator

- ID, class, and name locators

- `tagName` locator

- `linkText` and `partialLinkText` locators

- CSS and XPath locators

- JavaScript locators

Web pages are written in HyperText Markup Language (HTML for short). Cascading Style Sheets (CSS) beautify those pages. JavaScript brings the pages to life by giving them functionality. Any web page is a mix of those three foundational technologies. Note that Angular is not considered a substitute for XML/HTML. It is a development framework that gives more control over how data is dynamically manipulated and presented to the user on a web page. Applications and web pages built on Angular must use other technologies. Hence, you should know which operation should be applied to which element to interact or perform a function on it. And for that to happen, it is necessary to uniquely identify the element first. Since Angular offers enhancements to the DOM, there are some Angular-specific elements that are more easily located by Protractor than any other test framework's locator strategies.

© Shashank Shukla 2021
S. Shukla, *The Protractor Handbook*, https://doi.org/10.1007/978-1-4842-7289-3_2

I hope you now understand that good locator strategies are the foundation of any automation project. With the help of a good locator strategy, you can uniquely identify the element with which you need to interact with among numerous other elements present on a web page. *A good test script needs a uniquely identifiable element that remains unchanged throughout the developmental increments of the product to make the test script robust.* Let's now look at some locator strategies.

Tag Name

Let's take a slight detour to learn how to take a screenshot of a located element. The ability to take screenshots lets you accurately validate your results after successfully identifying elements.

Consider the web page shown in Figure 2-1. On the right side, you see Chrome DevTools docked on the web page. Chrome DevTools can inspect an element. Open it using Ctrl+Shift+I while you are on a web page.

If you open any web page in your browser and glance at the DOM, you find elements that do not have attributes like ID, class, or name readily available—these include elements like the <h1> tag, <td> tag, or <tr> tag. In these cases, you can use a tagName locator strategy. I captured the <h3> tag in Figure 2-1 because it's the only <h3> tag on the entire web site DOM, so I was guaranteed to get a unique element (i.e., heading 3).

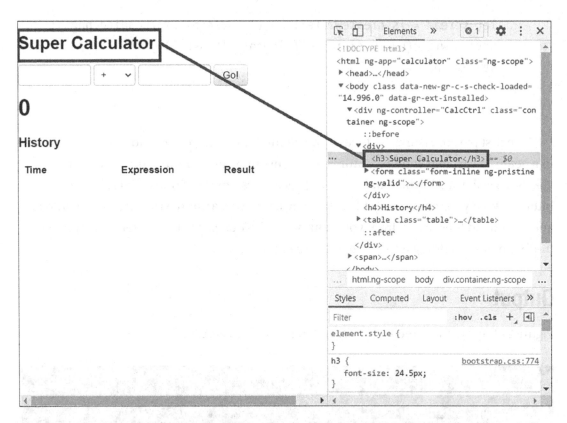

Figure 2-1. *Angular web page at* http://juliemr.github.io/protractor-demo/

Locating the element is not enough. You must also validate that the located element is correct and what you intended. Hence, let's capture its screenshot. First, create a folder named screenshot in your project's root directory. Then add the code in Listing 2-1 to the spec.js file inside the describe block.

Syntax

```
element(by.tagName('tagName'))
```

Listing 2-1. Locate an Element by Its Tagname and Capturing Its Screenshot

```
it('Should capture Element(tagName) Screenshot', function () {
    browser.get('http://juliemr.github.io/protractor-demo/');
    let heading = element(by.tagName('h3'))
    heading.takeScreenshot().then(function (element) {
```

```
        let stream = fs.createWriteStream('./screenshots/heading.png');
        stream.write(new Buffer.from(element, 'base64'));
        stream.end();
    })
})
```

The first part of Listing 2-1 locates the element by its tag name and stores it in a `heading` variable. It then captures a screenshot by using Protractor's browser `takeScreenshot` API, which uses the Node.js file system (`fs`) library. This library interacts with your computer's file system by creating read and write streams to upload and download files to and from your computer to Node.js. Do not forget to "`require`" the `fs` library by adding it to the first line of code.

Output

Figure 2-2 shows the screenshot is saved in the `screenshot` folder.

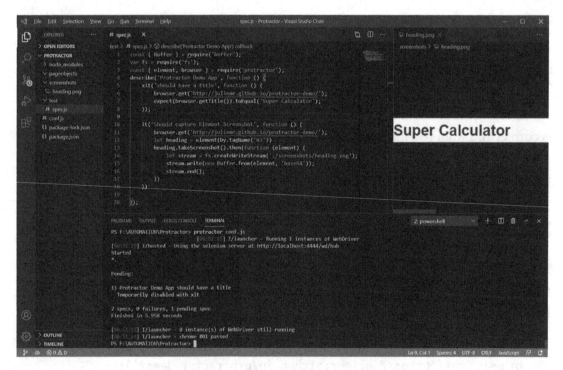

Figure 2-2. *Screenshot of h3 tag content saved on hard disk*

Note that if the tag is a button (e.g., something like `<button>Login</button>`), you can locate it by using the following customized locator strategy provided by Protractor.

```
element(by.buttonText('Log in')) or element(by.partialButtonText('Log'))
```

Table 2-1 lists differences between the syntax of traditional Java Selenium and the Protractor API in finding elements.

Table 2-1. *Syntax to Find Elements: Traditional Java Selenium vs. Protractor API*

Java Selenium	Protractor Customization
`driver.findElement(By.LocatorStrategy` `("LocatorValue"));`	`element(by.LocatorStrategy` `("LocatorValue");`
`driver.findElements(By.LocatorStrategy` `("LocatorValue"));`	`element.all(by.LocatorStrategy` `("LocatorValue");`

Depending on your Internet or CPU speed, the screenshot may not be captured, come out blurry, or be blank. To help with this, you can add a 10-second delay to the execution with `browser.sleep(10000)` just before taking the screenshot. This also gives you more time to slow down and observe the automated execution.

Next, let's look at other Selenium WebDriver inherited locator strategies in Protractor.

IDs

Refer to the element highlighted in Figure 2-3. `gobutton` is the Go button element ID that you want to capture. According to the World Wide Web Consortium (W3C), each element in the web page should have a unique ID. Although most dev teams don't follow this practice, they provide unique IDs to the most important elements, making this locator popular and highly reliable. Comment out (`xit`) from all previous `it` blocks before running the code in Listing 2-2; otherwise, you see multiple results after execution.

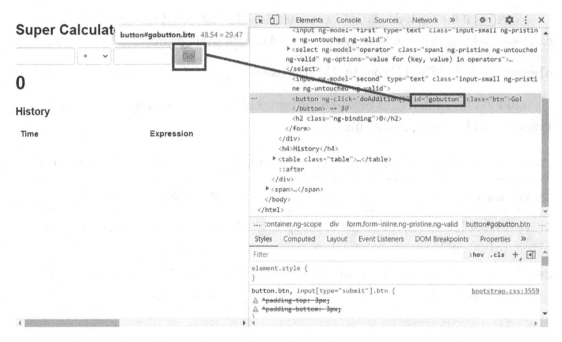

Figure 2-3. *Locating button by its ID*

Syntax

```
element(by.id('<idtext>'))
```

Listing 2-2. Finding an Element by ID

```
it('Should capture Element(id) Screenshot', function () {
    browser.get('http://juliemr.github.io/protractor-demo/');
    let button = element(by.id('gobutton'))
    button.takeScreenshot().then(function (element) {
        let stream = fs.createWriteStream('./screenshots/button.png');
        stream.write(new Buffer.from(element, 'base64'));
        stream.end();
    })
})
```

Output

In the console terminal window shown in Figure 2-4, **. represents two test cases that were skipped and one test case that passed. The test case execution time is 2.5 seconds. The later chapters provide an in-depth discussion of Protractor logs.

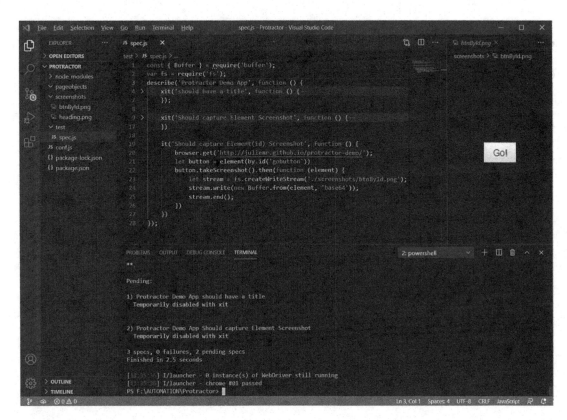

Figure 2-4. *Screenshot of Go! button on the right VS Code window using id locator strategy*

className

Figure 2-3 shows that the Go! HTML element that forms the Go button has another attribute. It is a class attribute with the value "btn". The `className` selector selects elements with a specific class attribute. Multiple elements in the HTML are grouped as a class to achieve consistency in formatting. Figure 2-3 is almost the same as Figure 2-2; the one difference is the `className` locator strategy is used in Listing 2-3 instead of the

ID locator strategy. Figure 2-5 shows that since the screenshot was saved, it implies that the element was first successfully located through the `className` selector. The screenshot functionality is an example; however, you can do anything with this element once it is located, such as get its text, send its text, or click it. You see other useful implementations in upcoming sections.

Syntax

```
element(by.className('<className>'))
```

Listing 2-3. Finding an Element by Class

```
it('Should capture Element(class) Screenshot', function () {
    browser.get('http://juliemr.github.io/protractor-demo/');
    let btn = element(by.className('btn'))
    btn.takeScreenshot().then(function (element) {
        let stream = fs.createWriteStream('./screenshots/btn_class.png');
        stream.write(new Buffer.from(element, 'base64'));
        stream.end();
    })
```

Output

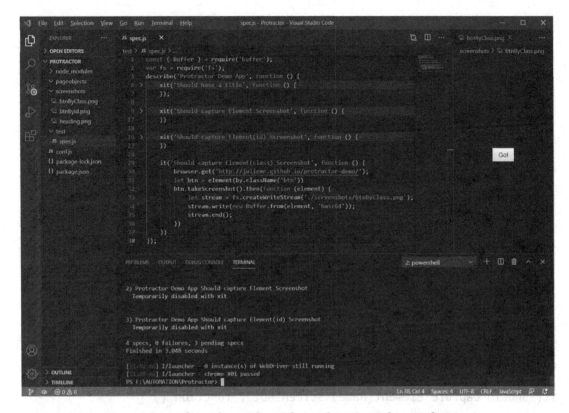

Figure 2-5. *Screenshot of Go! button on the right VS Code window using className locator strategy*

Name Attribute

You can only find the name attribute with following elements: `<a>`, `<applet>`, `<button>`, `<form>`, `<frame>`, `<iframe>`, `<img>`, `<input>`, `<map>`, `<meta>`, `<object>`, `<param>`, `<select>`, and `<textarea>`. You cannot find this attribute with `<span>` or `<div>`.

You can use this locator strategy to handle former elements as shown in Listing 2-4. Although it's rare to find the name attribute in an Angular web site, Figure 2-6 shows this attribute in the "Can't access your account?" link that is successfully located in Figure 2-7.

Figure 2-6. *Microsoft login page built on Angular as one of its techstacks*

Syntax

element(by.name('<name>'))

Listing 2-4. Finding an Element by Its Name Attribute

```
it('Should capture Element(name) Screenshot', function () {
    browser.get('https://login.microsoftonline.com/');
    browser.sleep(5000)
    let cantLogin = element(by.name('cannotAccessAccount'))
    cantLogin.takeScreenshot().then(function (element) {
        let stream = fs.createWriteStream('./screenshots/cantLogin.png');
        stream.write(new Buffer.from(element, 'base64'));
        stream.end();
    })
})
```

Output

Can't access your account?

Figure 2-7. *Screenshot of element using name locator strategy*

Link Text

Hyperlinks are rendered on a web page with an anchor (`<a>`) tag and accompanied by a link and text. If the anchor tag doesn't have a unique ID or name (see Figure 2-8), you can use the link text locator strategy from Listing 2-5 to fetch the result, as shown in Figure 2-9.

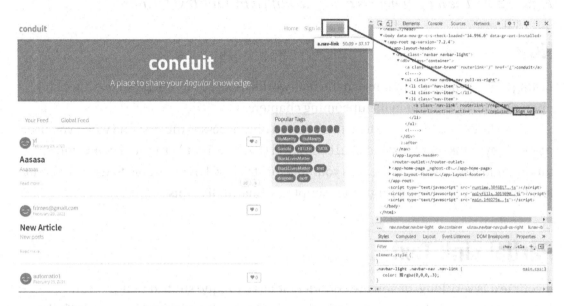

Figure 2-8. *Locating the element with its text Sign up*

Syntax

```
element(by.linkText('<linktext>'))
```

Listing 2-5. Finding an Element Using Link Text

```
it('Should capture Element(linkText) Screenshot', function () {
    browser.get('https://angular.realworld.io/');
    let signup = element(by.linkText('Sign up'))
    signup.takeScreenshot().then(function (element) {
        let stream = fs.createWriteStream('./screenshots/signup.png');
        stream.write(new Buffer.from(element, 'base64'));
        stream.end();
    })
})
```

Output

Sign up

Figure 2-9. *The output here is a link identified by LinkText locator*

Note

Listing 2-5 will make more sense in the real-world applications once you use the `click` operation on an element in the upcoming chapters.

If two links have the same text, this method only accesses the first one when you use `element(by.linkText)` instead of `element.all(by.linkText)`. To avoid confusion, bear this in mind when using link text as your locator strategy. It is advisable to use a different locator strategy for a more robust test script in scenarios like this.

Partial Link Text

If your text is very long, or you are confident it has a unique subtext that you can leverage (see Figure 2-10), use `Global` instead of `Global Feed` to uniquely identify the element through a partial link text locator strategy as shown in Listing 2-6. This ensures that your locators are not long and are easy to manage and more flexible when making any future changes to the link text and get you the saame result as show in Figure 2-11.

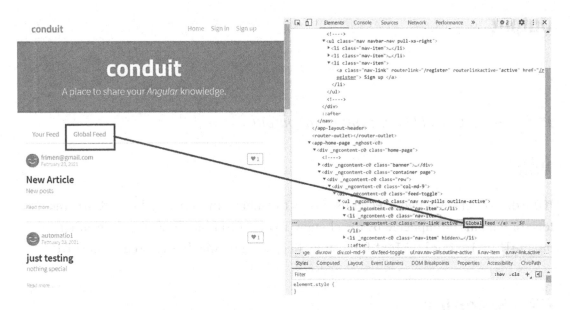

Figure 2-10. *Locating the element with its partial text i.e only Global*

Syntax

```
element(by.partialLinkText('<partiallinktext>'))
```

Listing 2-6. Finding an Element Using Partial Link Text

```
it('Should capture Element(partialLinkText) Screenshot', function () {
    browser.get('https://angular.realworld.io/');
    let globalFeed = element(by.partialLinkText('Global'))
    globalFeed.takeScreenshot().then(function (element) {
        let stream = fs.createWriteStream('./screenshots/globalFeed.png');
        stream.write(new Buffer.from(element, 'base64'));
        stream.end();
    })
})
```

Output

Global Feed

Figure 2-11. Global feed is captured as output

Note

If the developers ever need/tech businesses to rename an element, the `partialLinkText` locator remains unimpacted by the change. To avoid common mistakes, use either `partialLinkText` or `linkText` for testing. Keep in mind that both are case-sensitive.

CSS Selector

If you cannot find elements with general locators like ID, class, and name, use a CSS selector. Observe the element highlighted in Figure 2-12. It is a form with the `form-inline ng-pristine ng-valid` class. Listing 2-7 creates the CSS using the syntax shown in Figure 2-13. CSS selectors are a specific pattern through which you can uniquely locate an element in the DOM. CSS selectors select HTML elements according to their ID, class, type, or a combination of them to get a unique element, as shown in Figure 2-13.

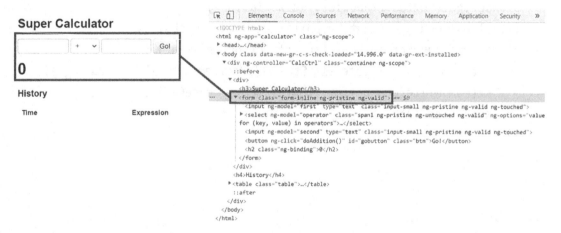

Figure 2-12. Form element

Syntax

```
element(by.css('tag[attribute="value"]'))
```

Listing 2-7. Creating CSS Using Syntax

```
it('Should capture Element(CSS) Screenshot', function () {
    browser.get('http://juliemr.github.io/protractor-demo/');
    let form = element(by.css('form[class="form-inline ng-pristine
    ng-valid"]'))
    form.takeScreenshot().then(function (element) {
        let stream = fs.createWriteStream('./screenshots/form.png');
        stream.write(new Buffer.from(element, 'base64'));
        stream.end();
    })
})
```

Output

0

Figure 2-13. *Form element and everything inside it is captured as output*

Note

cssContainingText is another CSS-based locator strategy. Protractor customizes it. Fetch the Go! button in Figure 2-12 using the following locator from Listing 2-7.

```
element(by.cssContainingText('.btn', 'Go!'))
```

On rare occasions when dealing with shadow elements, you can use the by.deepCss('value') locator.

XPath

XPath is short for XML Path Language, which navigates through the DOM of a web page. Developers use either CSS selectors or XPath locator strategies. It depends on which one is more familiar and comfortable or the strategy used by the organization for test automation.

Syntax

As you can see in Figure 2-14, XPath syntax starts with a double slash.

```
Xpath=//tagname[@attribute='value']
```

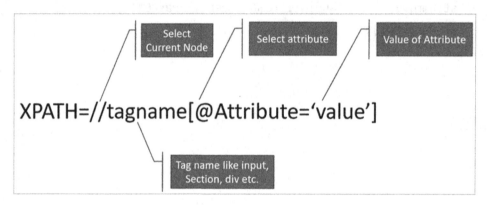

Figure 2-14. *XPath syntax*

// selects the current node. Tag names are any tag enclosed with angle brackets (<>), like div, form, p, or a. The @ symbol is a select attribute, like id, class, and ng-model. And value is the value of that attribute. Listing 2-8 fetches the Go! button, as depicted in Figure 2-15.

Listing 2-8. Finding an Element Through XPath

```
it('Should capture Element(xPath) Screenshot', function () {
    browser.get('http://juliemr.github.io/protractor-demo/');
    let btn = element(by.xpath('//button[@id="gobutton"]'))
    btn.takeScreenshot().then(function (element) {
        let stream = fs.createWriteStream('./screenshots/btn_xpath.png');
```

```
        stream.write(new Buffer.from(element, 'base64'));
        stream.end();
    })
})
```

Output

Figure 2-15. *Go! button identified by XPath*

Note

These days, CSS selectors are given preference over XPath because they are considered to be faster in the long run, especially if there are thousands of test scripts to run in a continuous integration environment. This is debatable. So as a best practice, you can ask the developers to add an ID to elements as much as possible, so you don't have to rely on XPath and CSS selectors all the time.

Go to www.w3schools.com/xml/xpath_syntax.asp for more information on how to use XPath.

Though it is always recommended that you should know how to use your own XPath syntax, there are some good online utilities, like the SelectorsHub add-on, that integrate with your browser. You can leverage it to find a selector (see Figure 2-16).

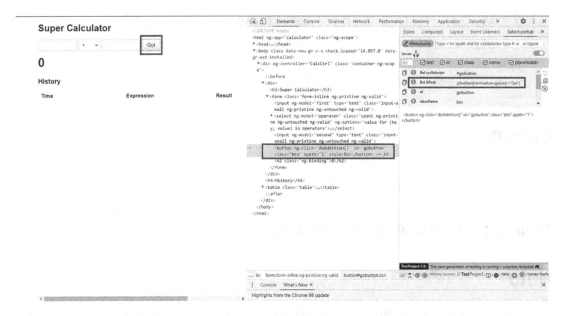

Figure 2-16. *SelectorsHub add-on window in Chrome developer tool*

JS Function

Protractor offers the flexibility of using vanilla JavaScript with a web-native API to fetch an element on a web page and successfully return it. Figure 2-17 highlights the Protractor logo. Listing 2-9 shows the unique way that this selector strategy can be integrated with Protractor and its result in Figure 2-18.

Figure 2-17. *Protractor logo from www.protractortest.org*

Syntax

```
document.querySelectorAll('.class or #id');
```

Listing 2-9. Finding an Element Through JavaScript

```
it('Should capture Element(JS) Screenshot', function () {
    browser.get('https://www.protractortest.org/');
    var img = element(by.js(function () {
        return document.querySelectorAll('.protractor-logo');
    }));

    img.takeScreenshot().then(function (element) {
        let stream = fs.createWriteStream('./screenshots/JS_logo.png');
        stream.write(new Buffer.from(element, 'base64'));
        stream.end();
    })
})
```

Output

Figure 2-18. *Protractor logo captured by JS document query locator*

The difference between WebDriver commands and JavaScript commands is when WebDriver does a click, it attempts as best as it can to simulate what happens when a real user uses the browser. Suppose the first element is a login <button> and the second element is transparent and completely covers the first element. When you tell WebDriver to click the first element, it simulates the click, but the second element (i.e., <div>) receives the click *first*. Why? Because the <div> element completely covers <button>, and if a user were to click <button>, then <div> would get the click event first. Whether or not the <button> element would eventually get the click event depends on how that transparent <div> handles the event. In this case, WebDriver's behavior is the same as when a real user tries to click a <button> element.

JavaScript's button.click() method does not reproduce what happens when a real user clicks <button>. JavaScript sends the click event directly to the <button> element, and the transparent <div> element doesn't get in its way.

You should make an informed decision on which option you choose as your locator strategy.

Summary

This concludes the discussion of non-Angular locator strategies. In this chapter, you learned different strategies inherited from the Selenium API to uniquely locate elements. The next chapter looks we look at additional locator strategies provided by Protractor to specifically handle Angular elements on a web page.

CHAPTER 3

Protractor Web Locators

This chapter shows you how to locate elements on a web page using Protractor-provided customized locator strategies to handle Angular elements. You will about learn the following.

- Dealing with more than one fetched element

- Angular locators like `model`, `repeater`, and `binding`

- `exactRepeater` and `exactBinding` locators

- `buttonText` and `partialButtonText` locators

- `optionsOptions`

Fetching More Than One Element

In test automation, you often fetch more than one element, depending on the selector you use. For instance, in Figure 3-1, there are three elements identified by the `<th>` tag after using the `document.getElementsByTagName('th')` function. If you want to capture any one of these elements, you must first capture all of them in a variable. You can do it by using the `element.all` API provided by Protractor, as shown in Listing 3-1.

© Shashank Shukla 2021

S. Shukla, *The Protractor Handbook*, https://doi.org/10.1007/978-1-4842-7289-3_3

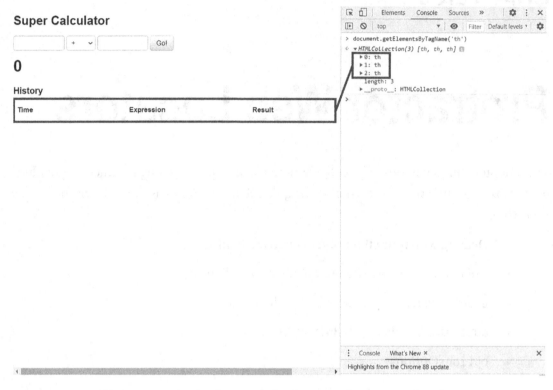

Figure 3-1. *All elements in the Super Calculator web page with <th> tag*

Syntax

```
element.all(by.tagName('value'))
```

Listing 3-1. Fetching Multiple Elements

```
it('Should capture Multiple Elements', function () {
    browser.get('http://juliemr.github.io/protractor-demo/');
    let elems = element.all(by.tagName('th'))
    elems.then(function (item) {
        console.log("Count of <th> elements is:  " + item.length)
    })
})
```

Output

Figure 3-2 shows the "Count of <th> elements is: 3" output in the console terminal. If you are skipping the earlier test cases using xit, you find them denoted by an asterisk (*) in the console terminal.

```
PS F:\AUTOMATION\Protractor> protractor conf.js
[03:30:40] I/launcher - Running 1 instances of WebDriver
[03:30:40] I/hosted - Using the selenium server at http://localhost:4444/wd/hub
Started
*********Count of <th> elements is:  3
```

Figure 3-2. *Output of earlier skipped tests and count of <th> elements*

It is critical to understand what is going on in Listing 3-1—especially the .then part. The first two lines of code open the web page. They then find all <th> elements and store them in the elems variable, respectively. Since the elems variable holds more than one element, it has to be an array.

Thankfully, Protractor manages all the asynchronous JavaScript operations for its APIs, so the user doesn't need to worry about the execution sequence during automation.

console.log, however, is a native JavaScript function, and Protractor can't hold it from being executed, even if its predecessor lines of code take a while to get a response from the server (Selenium and the browser). Hence, you must forcefully make the execution sequential and hold the console.log statement from running until its previous line of code is executed. This is done by chaining it with the help of the .then function. In other words, you make the console.log("Count of <th> elements is: " + item.length) step to exclusively wait for the let elems = element.all(by. tagName('th')) step to complete as it fetches the elements from the Selenium server and the browser. You are ensuring that all the elements are first fetched, and only then can they be printed in the terminal by the console.log statement.

Another observation is that item.length is used rather than elems.length. The code before the .then function executes the result fetched by that code is passed to the THEN function via the item variable. You can choose any variable name other than item, and the code works just fine. So the fetched elems array is passed to the .then function via the `item` variable. Then you count the number of elements fetched using the JavaScript on the `item` variable. You see its Protractor equivalent later in the book, which makes developers' lives easier by avoiding the use of `.then` promise handling.

For more information on JavaScript's asynchronous features, refer to www.geeksforgeeks.org/why-you-use-then-method-in-javascript.

Chain Selectors

Sometimes narrowing down on an element helps locate it uniquely in a DOM as it shrinks the scope of the search. As soon as a locator is chained to another locator, its scope is confined to its predecessor's child elements. You can filter out irrelevant elements by forming multiple chained element locator queries. Open your browser and match the Conduit web page DOM (see Figure 3-3). There are 57 `<li>` elements on the web page. You can validate this through Protractor from the first part of the output in Listing 3-2 (see Figure 3-5).

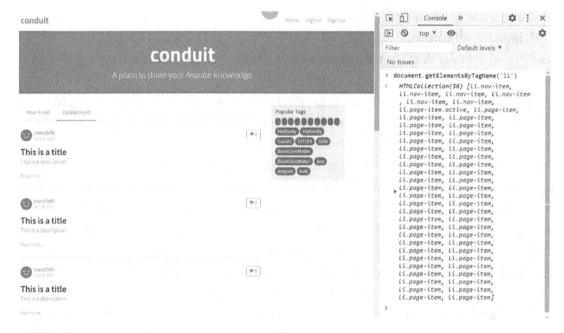

Figure 3-3. *57 <li> present in the entire web page*

Out of these 57 <li> tags, how many are available inside the web site Navbar? Figure 3-4 shows the number of <li> elements present underneath the Navbar's <ul> tag with the nav navbar-nav pull-xs-right class. With a cursory glance, you can figure out that under the Navbar's <ul> tag, there are only three <li> elements present. Figure 3-2 shows that you can uniquely locate the Navbar and then chain another element.all locator to find all the <li> tags located underneath that Navbar.

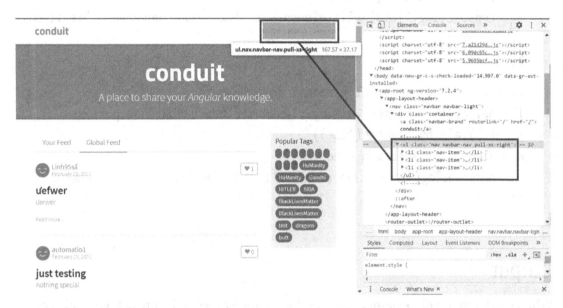

Figure 3-4. *Three <li> present under Navbar's <ul> element*

Syntax

```
element.all(by.selector('value')).all(by.selector('value')))
//multiple elements array
element(by.selector('value')).element(by.selector('value')))
//single element
element.all(by.selector('value')).element(by.selector('value')))
//single element
element(by.selector('value')).all(by.selector('value')))
//multiple elements array
```

Listing 3-2. Chaining Locators in Protractor

```
it('Should capture Elements through chaining locators', function () {
    browser.get('https://angular.realworld.io/');
    //Part 1: Finding all LI elements in a webpage
    let elems = element.all(by.tagName('li'))
    elems.then(function (item) {
        console.log("Total <li> elements in the entire Webpage:   " + item.
        length)
    })

    //Part 2: Finding all LI elements in a Navbar
    let nav_elems = element.all(by.className('nav navbar-nav pull-xs-
    right')).all(by.tagName('li'))
    nav_elems.then(function (item) {
        console.log("Total <li> elements inside Navbar:   " + item.length)
    })
})
```

Output

When you fetch the <li> elements under the Navbar shown in Figure 3-4, you only get three, as seen in Figure 3-5.

```
[13:49:10] I/launcher - 0 instance(s) of WebDriver still running
[13:49:10] I/launcher - chrome #01 passed
PS F:\AUTOMATION\Protractor> protractor conf.js
[14:01:16] I/launcher - Running 1 instances of WebDriver
[14:01:16] I/hosted - Using the selenium server at http://localhost:4444/wd/hub
Started
**********Total <li> elements in the entire Webpage:   57
Total <li> elements inside Navbar:   3
```

Figure 3-5. *Element identified as a result of chaining locators*

Upcoming chapters investigate how to narrow the scope of search down to only one uniquely identifiable element that an action can be performed on.

Model

Let's look at Angular-specific locator strategies. A web page made from Angular technology has some additional Angular-specific elements in its DOM to ensure a better and smoother rendition. Figure 3-6 shows the input element rendered at `http://juliemr.github.io/protractor-demo/`.

Figure 3-6. *ng-model Angular locator*

Listing 3-3 fetches the second input box, which is seen in Figure 3-7.

Syntax

```
element(by.model('value'));
```

Listing 3-3. Capturing ng-model with Protractor

```
it('Should capture Angular Element(model) Screenshot', function () {
    browser.get('http://juliemr.github.io/protractor-demo/');
    let inputbox = element(by.model('second'));
    inptbx.takeScreenshot().then(function (element) {
        let stream = fs.createWriteStream('./screenshots/second_inputbox.
        png');
        stream.write(new Buffer.from(element, 'base64'));
        stream.end();
    })
})
```

Output

Figure 3-7. *Element screenshot fetched by ng-model Angular locator*

Repeater and exactRepeater

The ng-repeat directive in Angular repeats the HTML code for a given number of times. ng-repeat is an iterator like the forEach loop in JavaScript. The following data is an example.

```
$scope.planets = [
{id: 1, name: "Mercury"},
{id: 2, name: "Venus"},
{id: 3, name: "Earth"},
{id: 4, name: "Mars"},
{id: 5, name: "Jupiter"},
];
```

If you want this data to render in the DOM as a table with each item as a separate row, you can use ng-repeat to do it in Angular, as shown next.

```
< tr ng-repeat="planet in planets" class="item" >
<td>{{planet.id}}</td>
<td>{{planet.name}}</td>
</tr >
```

I urge you to manually observe this by launching a browser and visiting the Super Calculator web page. Click the Go! button a few times and observe how the dynamic DOM changes inside the <tbody> tag and new <tr> elements are rendered (see Figure 3-8).

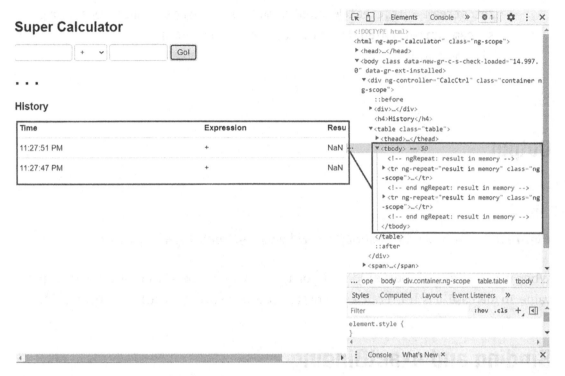

Figure 3-8. *ng-repeat in action*

Let's try to capture it by using Protractor. In Listing 3-4, after landing on the Super Calculator web page, locate and click the Go! button using one of the element APIs of Protractor called .click() to imitate a user mouse-click action. This triggers the repeater to render the first <tr> element inside the <tbody> tag, as shown in Figure 3-8. In the next step, you locate and capture this first element, as shown in Figure 3-9.

Syntax

```
element(by.repeater('value'))
```

Listing 3-4. Capturing ng-model with Protractor

```
it('Should capture Angular Element(repeater) Screenshot', function () {
    browser.get('http://juliemr.github.io/protractor-demo/');
    element(by.id('gobutton')).click()
    let tr = element(by.repeater('memory'))
    tr.takeScreenshot().then(function (element) {
```

```
        let stream = fs.createWriteStream('./screenshots/table_repeat.png');
        stream.write(new Buffer.from(element, 'base64'));
        stream.end();
    })
})
```

Output

11:52:20 PM   +   NaN

Figure 3-9. *Element screenshot fetched by ng-repeater Angular locator*

When using the exactRepeater locator, you must provide the exact string as the ng-repeat value. In this case, it is let tr = element(by.exactRepeater('result in memory')).

Binding and exactBinding

The ng-bind directive tells Angular to dynamically replace an HTML element's content with the result of a given variable or expression. The first thing to remember when dealing with binding is that it is not a value. It is an expression or variable that is executed during the DOM formation. Let's build upon the last example and see if you can locate and capture the result on the screen. If you observe Figure 3-10, you find that the element looks like just any other element in the DOM.

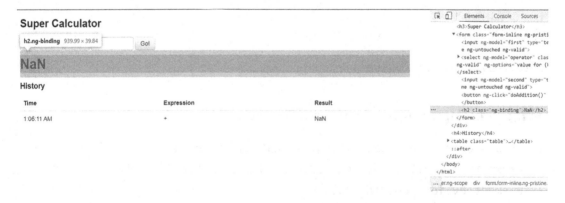

Figure 3-10. *<h2> element showing the result of the latest operation*

When you right-click the page and then click View Page Source in Chrome, however, you notice that the actual expression responsible for generating this value is very different, as highlighted in Figure 3-11.

```
1   <!DOCTYPE HTML>
2   <html ng-app="calculator">
3   <head>
4       <script src="https://ajax.googleapis.com/ajax/libs/angularjs/1.3.0/angular.min.js"></script>
5       <script src="./calc.js"></script>
6       <link href="./bootstrap.css" rel="stylesheet">
7       <title>Super Calculator</title>
8   </head>
9   <body class="ng-cloak">
10      <div ng-controller="CalcCtrl" class="container">
11          <div>
12              <h3>Super Calculator</h3>
13              <form class="form-inline">
14                  <input ng-model="first" type="text" class="input-small"/>
15                  <select ng-model="operator" class="span1"
16                          ng-options="value for (key, value) in operators">
17                  </select>
18                  <input ng-model="second" type="text" class="input-small"/>
19                  <button ng-click="doAddition()" id="gobutton" class="btn">Go!</button>
20                  <h2>{{latest}}</h2>
21              </form>
22          </div>
23          <h4>History</h4>
24          <table class="table">
25              <thead><tr>
26                  <th>Time</th>
27                  <th>Expression</th>
28                  <th>Result</th>
29              </tr></thead>
30              <tr ng-repeat="result in memory">
31                  <td>
32                      {{result.timestamp | date:'mediumTime'}}
33                  </td>
34                  <td>
35                      <span>{{result.first}}</span>
36                      <span>{{result.operator}}</span>
37                      <span>{{result.second}}</span>
38                  </td>
39                  <td>{{result.value}}</td>
40              </tr>
41          </table>
42      </div>
43  </body>
44  </html>
```

Figure 3-11. *Source code responsible for rendering <h2> on web page*

Listing 3-5 captures the `<h2>` element by its real value (i.e., latest) and displays it, as seen in Figure 3-12.

Syntax

```
element(by.binding('value'))
```

Listing 3-5. Capturing ng-bind with Protractor

```
it('Should capture Angular Element(binding) Screenshot', function () {
    browser.get('http://juliemr.github.io/protractor-demo/');
    element(by.id('gobutton')).click();
    let result = element(by.binding('latest'));
```

```
    result.takeScreenshot().then(function (element) {
        let stream = fs.createWriteStream('./screenshots/result.png');
        stream.write(new Buffer.from(element, 'base64'));
        stream.end();
    })
})
```

Output

NaN

Figure 3-12. Output of latest equation in <h2> on web page

In JavaScript, NaN means the value is "Not-a-Number," or the number is not valid or legal. Here, it is an expected result, as you are adding two blanks that have generated the NaN result.

On your own, try to figure out the difference between binding and exactBinding, and capture the elements corresponding to the following HTML snippets in the Super Calculator web app.

```
<span>{{result.first}}</span>
<span>{{result.operator}}</span>
<span>{{result.second}}</span>
```

Options

This locator is specifically customized to handle drop-down elements on a web page. It has a distinct appearance and can be identified during a cursory glance at the DOM. Figure 3-13 highlights a drop-down element on the Super Calculator web page.

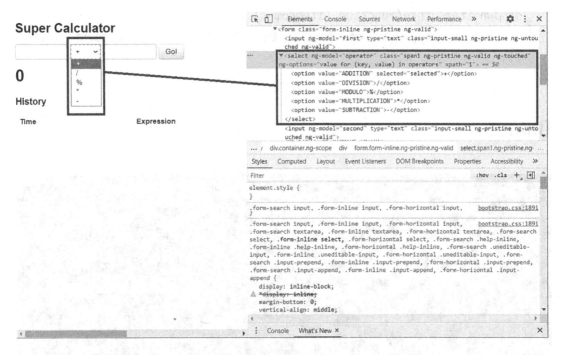

Figure 3-13. *<select> tag for drop-down*

Let's determine the number of drop-down elements. Listing 3-6 captures a drop-down element using the Options selector strategy and stores it in `drpdwn_items`. In the next step, you chain it with the `.then` function, which eventually waits for the previous step to complete. The result received via the `itemcount` variable is printed in the `console.log` of the terminal, as shown in Figure 3-14.

Syntax

```
element.all(by.options('value'));
```

Listing 3-6. Capturing ng-options with Protractor

```
it('Should capture drop-down Element(options) count', function () {
    browser.get('http://juliemr.github.io/protractor-demo/');
    let drpdwn_items = element.all(by.options('value for (key, value) in
    operators'))
```

```
    drpdwn_items.then(function (itemcount) {
        console.log("Count of items in the drop-down:  " + itemcount.length)
    })
})
```

Output

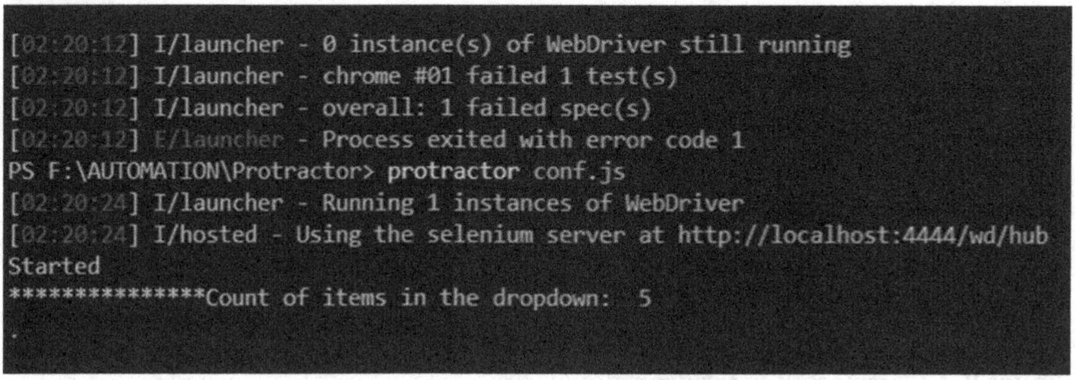

Figure 3-14. *Console output of the number of elements/items in the drop-down*

Custom Selectors

Observe the highlighted element on Protractor's official web page, as shown in
Figure 3-15. If you want to locate all four elements in the highlighted drop-down
menu, you must use a CSS selector as your locator strategy, such as element.all(by.
css('a[tabindex="-1"]')). What if the tabindex attribute were used with the <div>
tag? Or what if this type of HTML element was used on a large scale in the app? At some
point, you find using this locator strategy hard to maintain. You would ask yourself,
"Why can't I use the tabindex attribute like the 'class'(by.class) attribute?" It turns
out you can. You can create your own custom locators with the help of JavaScript query
selectors in Protractor.

Figure 3-15. *Number of elements inside a drop-down*

The first part of Listing 3-7 defines the custom locator strategy using the `addLocator` API. Ideally, you should have placed it inside the `onPrepare` hook, but let's keep that discussion for later chapters. The latter part of Listing 3-7 calls this custom locator to fetch all the elements that the locator can fetch in the web page, which would not have been possible with any of the existing locator strategies.

Syntax

`by.addLocator()`

Listing 3-7. Custom Locators

```
it('Should fetch all elements with attribute "tabindex"', function () {

    by.addLocator('tabindex', function (value, parentElement) {
        parentElement = parentElement || document;
        var nodes = parentElement.querySelectorAll('[tabindex]');
        return Array.prototype.filter.call(nodes, function (node) {
            return (node.getAttribute('tabindex') === value);
        });
    });
```

```
browser.get('https://www.protractortest.org/#/');
var tabindexes = element.all(by.tabindex('-1'));
tabindexes.then(function (item) {
    console.log("Count of elements with attribute 'tabindex' is:  " +
    item.length)
})
});
```

Output

The count of 26 elements fetched in Figure 3-16 matches the number of elements fetched by the search bar in Chrome DevTools in Figure 3-15.

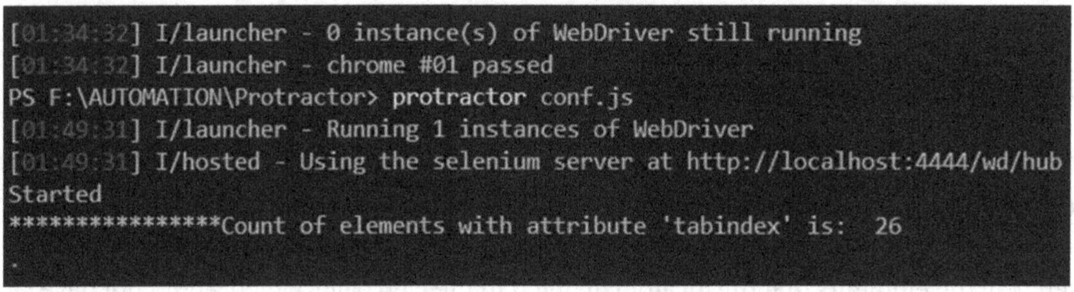

Figure 3-16. *Count of elements with tabindex value = –1*

Summary

This concludes the discussion on Angular locator strategies. In this chapter, you learned different strategies to uniquely locate elements. After identifying the elements, you capture their screenshots or count them. In real-life automation projects, these two operations are only a fraction of the overall operations that you must do on identified elements. Many other operations are done in the real world, from simple functions like click, get text, and insert text to more complex ones like drag-and-drop, selecting from drop-down menus, and handling browser pop-ups.

The next chapter looks at various browser API commands, starting with the simple ones provided by Protractor to interact with the located elements.

CHAPTER 4

Web Page Interactions I

Now that you know how to install the Protractor tool and uniquely locate elements on a web page, the next step is to interact or perform actions on the located elements. In this chapter, you see how to perform various actions on the located elements in a web page. You learn various API commands to interact with these elements and how Protractor implements them with ease. You about learn the following.

- Comparing `async`/`await` and `then`

- Debugging

- Simple tasks like

    - Getting an element's text

    - Sending text to an element

    - Click, double-click, and right-click user actions

    - Element count

    - Fetching the first, last, or any element from an array of elements

    - Iterating all elements of an array

Browser APIs are built into your web browser and can expose data from it. Protractor provides a set of easy-to-understand commands that wrap browser APIs to perform various tasks.

Let's look at some of the activities that can be performed on a web page and their respective Protractor syntax and implementation.

© Shashank Shukla 2021
S. Shukla, *The Protractor Handbook*, https://doi.org/10.1007/978-1-4842-7289-3_4

Understanding then and async/await

Understanding the basic concepts of JavaScript's asynchronous behavior is imperative when dealing with Protractor's browser APIs. JavaScript is a single-threaded language (i.e., it can process only one statement at a time). This means that if your statement intends to fetch some data from the server, such as fetching the header text of a web page, it must block the entire execution until the server provides the requested data. To overcome this, JavaScript was inherently designed to be asynchronous. That means it uses certain mechanisms (callbacks, promises, async-await) that ensure that the execution continues without waiting for the server response, and once the response is fetched, the control can come back to that specific statement and execute it.

Open a web browser and its developer tools and paste the code provided in Listing 4-1 in the console. The setTimeout() method calls a function or evaluates an expression after a specified number of milliseconds; that is, it blocks the execution for a specified period of time.

Listing 4-1. Understanding Order of Execution

```
function first() { setTimeout(function () { console.log("First I print") },
500); }

function second() { console.log("Then I print") }
```

Figure 4-1 shows that when you execute these functions in a specific order, even though the first() function is placed before the second() function in the code, JavaScript won't let the delay of 500 milliseconds block the entire execution. It will go on and execute the next statement ('second()') before first statement ('first()') and return back in 500 milliseconds to execute the first() function.

Figure 4-1. *Asynchronous order of execution of JavaScript*

This asynchronous nature of JavaScript/Node.js is a good feature for dealing with server responses. However, in automation, a strict order of execution of the test statements is easier to understand. So, how do you make the function `first()` in the Listing 4-1 blocking thus making the code synchronous? By using the `Promise` API's '.then' function.

Listing 4-1 is synchronized into Listing 4-2 by chaining it to a `.then` function.

Listing 4-2. Synchronizing the Code with the Help of Promise

```
function first() {
    return new Promise(function (resolve, reject) {
        setTimeout(() => {
            resolve("First I print");
        }, 500);

    });
};

function second() {
    return new Promise(function (resolve, reject) {
        resolve("Then I print");
    });
};
```

```
first().then(function (resolvedfromfirst) {
    console.log(resolvedfromfirst);
    return second();
}).then(function (resolvedfromsecond) {
    console.log(resolvedfromsecond);
})
```

It is bewildering to look at the mess that has to be made to synchronize two statements. JavaScript is an evolving language, and there are a lot of benefits of asynchronous coding—especially while dealing with servers—that justify the complex syntax as a fair trade-off. Even if you are very new to coding, match the syntax in Listing 4-2 to Listing 4-1 and try to make sense out of the differences. Note the output received in Figure 4-2 and match it with the syntax of all the .then functions used in earlier tests.

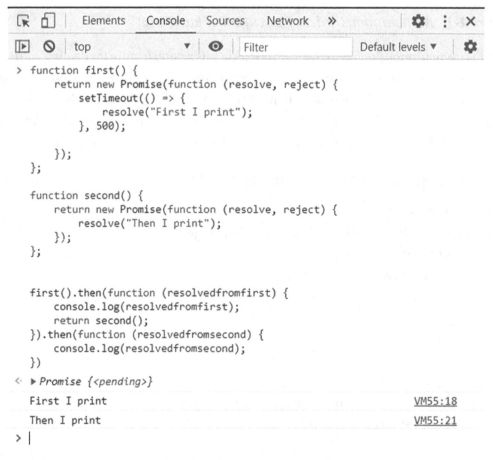

Figure 4-2. *Synchronous order of execution of JavaScript using promises*

It takes patience, practice, and more investigation of the code to familiarize yourself with it.   •

For more information on promises, refer to https://developer.mozilla.org/ en-US/docs/Web/JavaScript/Reference/Global_Objects/Promise.

However, things do get better with the introduction of async/await. It manages the promises and ensures a synchronous execution like .then but with a simpler syntax. Listing 4-3 is a conversion of Listing 4-2 using async/await syntax.

Previously, the Protractor control-flow mechanism arranged the test steps/lines of code in a sequence and maintained the order of execution. Now, synchronization and order of execution are handled by async/await. So, you should disable the control-flow by adding SELENIUM_PROMISE_MANAGER: false, to the conf.js file and add async/await to the code from here on.

Listing 4-3. Synchronizing the Code with async/await

```javascript
function first() {
    return new Promise(function (resolve, reject) {
        setTimeout(() => {
            resolve("First I print");
        }, 500);

    });
};

function second() {
    return new Promise(function (resolve, reject) {
        resolve("Then I print");
    });
};

async function printAll() {
    console.log(await first());
    console.log(await second());

}
```

The clarity of the code and the result obtained is the same, as seen in Figure 4-3.

```
  ⌧  ⬚  │   Elements   Console   Sources   Network   »          ⚙  ⋮  ✕

  ▷  ⊘  │  top              ▼  ◉  │ Filter           Default levels ▼  │  ⚙

 >  function first() {
        return new Promise(function (resolve, reject) {
            setTimeout(() => {
                resolve("First I print");
            }, 500);

        });
    };
    function second() {
        return new Promise(function (resolve, reject) {
            resolve("Then I print");
        });
    };



    async function printAll(){
        console.log(await first());
        console.log(await second());

    }

    printAll()
 ‹· ▶ Promise {<pending>}

    First I print                                        VM535:19
    Then I print                                         VM535:20
 >
```

Figure 4-3. *Synchronous order of execution of JavaScript using async/await*

For more information on `async/await`, refer to `https://developer.mozilla.org/en-US/docs/Learn/JavaScript/Asynchronous/Async_await`.

Debugging

Before learning about browser APIs, you need to understand how to debug your script. Visual Studio Code has built-in debugging support for the Node.js runtime and can debug JavaScript, TypeScript, and any other language that is transpiled to JavaScript. You can set up Visual Studio Code to debug Protractor scripts in four simple steps.

As shown in Figure 4-4, first, click the Debugging icon. Next, click "create a `launch.json` file." Then, select the Node.js option in the drop-down.

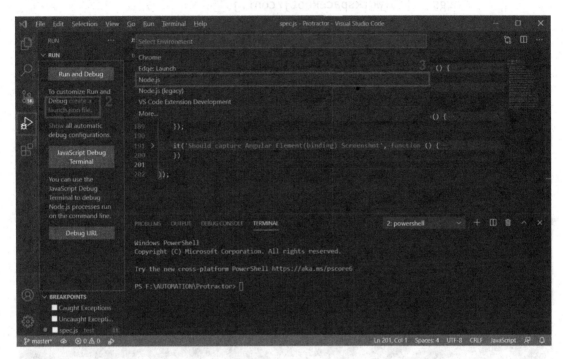

Figure 4-4. *Visual Studio Code debugger*

Copy the code from Listing 4-4 and replace it with the entire code present in the newly created `launch.json` file, and save it.

Listing 4-4. launch.json

```
{
    "version": "0.2.0",
    "configurations": [

        {
            "type": "pwa-node",
            "request": "launch",
            "name": "Protractor Debugger",
            "skipFiles": [
```

```
            "<node_internals>/**"
        ],
        "program": "${workspaceRoot}/node_modules/protractor/bin/
        protractor",
        "args": ["${workspaceRoot}/conf.js"],
    }
  ]
}
```

The name, type, and request parameters in the launch.json file are standard.
Ensure that the value of the key program is the path for the node_modules\protractor\
bin\protractor file in your workspace. The args value should be the path of your
Protractor config file in your workspace. Your launch.json file setup should look like
Figure 4-5.

Figure 4-5. *Project instance after launch.json file setup is complete*

Start the Selenium server with webdriver-manager start if it's not already running.
Hover over the line number in the spec.js file where you intend to pause the execution,
and set the breakpoint by clicking the red dot as soon as it appears. This ensures that
your execution halts at that step and provides you time to analyze your code and the
elements on the web page until you press the Continue button or hit F5.

Start your execution by clicking the green play button named Protractor Debugger. You can use the controls provided by the debugger to navigate the execution while the debugger is running (see Figure 4-6).

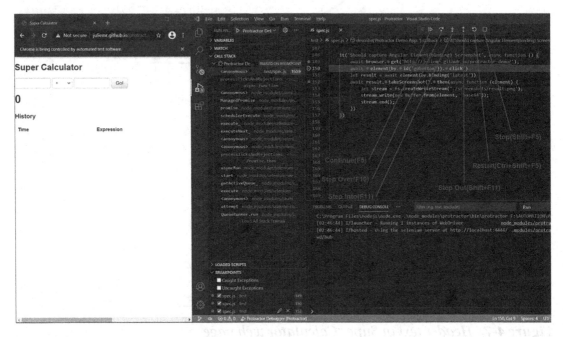

Figure 4-6. *Debugger controls*

Notes

Go to `https://code.visualstudio.com/docs/nodejs/nodejs-debugging` for more information on debugging with Visual Studio Code.

Get an Element's Text

Getting text from a web page is one of the basic actions that users perform. Most of the element types on a web page contain the text in tags; for instance, `<p>`, `<a>`, `<span>`, `<li>`, all the heading tags—`<h1>` to `<h6>` (see Figure 4-7), and many more. The `<div>` tag is often used to group block-level elements to format them with styles but can technically accommodate plain text as well.

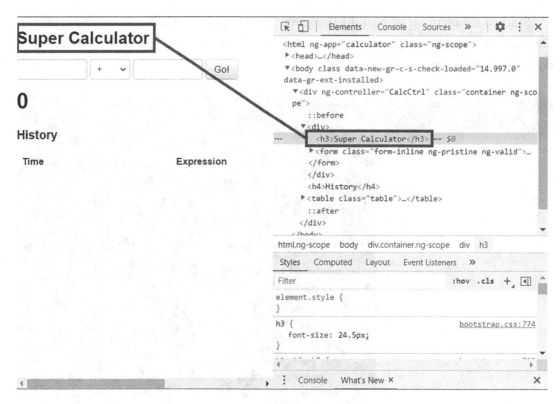

Figure 4-7. *Header text in Super Calculator web page*

Listing 4-5 fetches the text of the header element <h3> on the web page. Once you land on the page, you locate and store the text of <h3> in the header variable. The content of the header variable is a promise since element().getText() returns a Promise object that is managed by await and is eventually printed by console.log in the final statement.

Syntax

```
element(by.tagName('value')).getText();
```

Listing 4-5. Getting Text of the Header Element on the Web Page

```
it('Should capture text and print it in console', async function () {
    await browser.get('http://juliemr.github.io/protractor-demo/');
    let heading = await element(by.tagName('h3')).getText();
    console.log("The Heading of the Web page is:- " + heading)
})
```

Output

Figure 4-8 shows the console output.

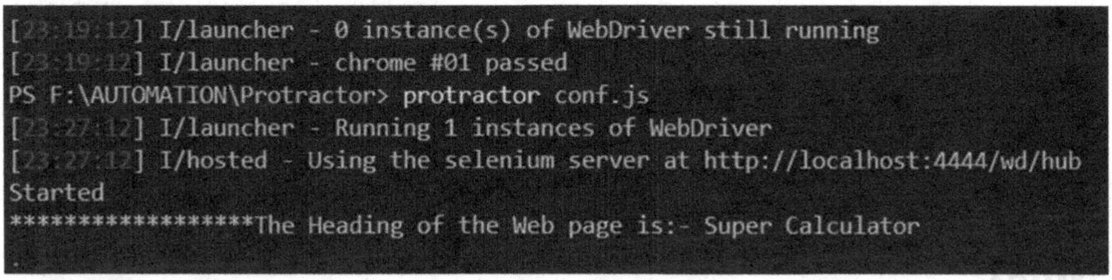

Figure 4-8. *Header text in Super Calculator web page*

Notes

Try to print the header variable in the console without using the .then function and observe the output. You see the output as [object Object] because you are trying to return an object (element) as a string. Since there is no better vocabulary to represent an object as a string, the object's console.log value is set to [object Object] by the JavaScript engine.

Send Text to an Input Field

SendKeys command in Listing 4-6 sends the text to the input fields on the Super Calculator web page (see Figure 4-9).

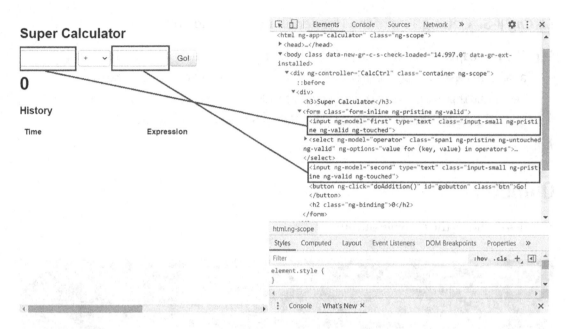

Figure 4-9. *Input fields in Super Calculator web page*

Syntax

```
element(by.locator('value')).sendKeys('value');
```

Listing 4-6. Sending a String to \<input\> Tags

```
it('Should send the text to input field of the web page', async function () {
    await browser.get('http://juliemr.github.io/protractor-demo/');
    await element(by.model('first')).sendKeys('5');
    await element(by.model('second')).sendKeys('8');
    await browser.takeScreenshot().then(function (fullpage) {
        var stream = fs.createWriteStream('./screenshots/page_ss.png');
        stream.write(new Buffer.from(fullpage, 'base64'));
        stream.end();
    })
})
```

Output

The screenshot is captured and saved in the screenshots folder, as shown in Figure 4-10.

Figure 4-10. *Screenshot of the web page after sending text to input boxes*

Notes

SendKeys command always clears any existing value in the input box, and then sends the text to it. Special characters and keystrokes like Alt, Ctrl, and Enter can also be sent to the web page. The following line of code sends the Enter key to a web page.

```
element(by.locator('value')).sendKeys(protractor.Key.ENTER);
```

Go to www.selenium.dev/selenium/docs/api/javascript/module/selenium-webdriver/index_exports_Key.html for a list of the available options.

Click an Element

You can use this simple Click command to automate mouse clicks by a user on a web page. Let's use Listing 4-6 and enhance it by adding the click() function, as shown in Listing 4-7. Four seconds were applied to browser.sleep() to pause the execution because it takes a few seconds to display the result (see Figure 4-11).

Syntax

```
element(by.locator('value')).click()
```

Listing 4-7. Left-Click Function

```
it('Should click the "Go!" button on web page', async function () {
    await browser.get('http://juliemr.github.io/protractor-demo/');
    await element(by.model('first')).sendKeys('5');
    await element(by.model('second')).sendKeys('8');
    await element(by.id('gobutton')).click();
    await browser.sleep(3000)
    browser.takeScreenshot().then(function (fullpage) {
        var stream = fs.createWriteStream('./screenshots/page_click.png');
        stream.write(new Buffer.from(fullpage, 'base64'));
        stream.end();
    })
})
```

Output

Time	Expression	Result
2:56:44 AM	5 + 8	13

Figure 4-11. *Result captured 3 seconds after clicking the Go! button*

Double-Click an Element

Unlike a single click, the double-click operation is provided by the Actions class in Selenium. Complex browser interactions like drag-and-drop and double-click, which cannot be done with simple WebElement commands, are handled by the Actions class, as shown in Listing 4-8.

Syntax

```
browser.actions().doubleClick("locator").perform()
```

Listing 4-8. Double-Clicking an Element

```
it('Should double click the "Go!" button on web page', async function () {
    await browser.get('http://juliemr.github.io/protractor-demo/');
    await element(by.model('first')).sendKeys('5');
    await element(by.model('second')).sendKeys('8');
    let go_btn = await element(by.id('gobutton'));
    await browser.actions().doubleClick(go_btn).perform()
    await browser.sleep(3000)
    await browser.takeScreenshot().then(function (fullpage) {
        var stream = fs.createWriteStream('./screenshots/
        page_dbclick.png');
        stream.write(new Buffer.from(fullpage, 'base64'));
        stream.end();
    })
})
```

Output

In Figure 4-12, the first result is 13; however, since the second click is made almost at the same time as the first click, the timestamp is the same, and the result is NaN since there was no input before the second click.

Super Calculator

NaN

History

Time	Expression	Result
3:16:18 AM	+	NaN
3:16:18 AM	5 + 8	13

Figure 4-12. *Result captured after double-clicking the Go button*

Right-Click an Element

You can also right-click an element by using the parameters provided in the click method under the Actions class, as shown in Listing 4-9. However, at the time of writing this book, there is an open issue with this functionality, and the right-click user action is not simulated. Please refer to https://github.com/angular/protractor/issues/5271 and https://github.com/angular/protractor/issues/5391 for the latest updates.

Syntax

```
browser.actions().click(<locator>, protractor.Button.RIGHT).perform();
```

Listing 4-9. Right-Clicking an Element

```
it('Should right click the "Go!" button on web page', async function () {
    await browser.get('http://juliemr.github.io/protractor-demo/');
    let go_btn = await element(by.id('gobutton'));
    await browser.actions().click(go_btn, protractor.Button.RIGHT).
    perform();
    await browser.sleep(5000)
})
```

Output

As a workaround, if you add the highlighted piece of code in your conf.js configuration file, you can still use Click API. You will learn more about capabilities later in the book.

```
exports.config = {
    framework: 'jasmine',
    seleniumAddress: 'http://localhost:4444/wd/hub',
    specs: ['test/spec.js'],
    capabilities: {
        'browserName': 'chrome',
```

```
    'chromeOptions': {
        w3c: false
    },
  },
}
```

Since a right-click is a C language web browser function, it is not captured as part of the web page screenshot. Hence, you can observe it using `browser.sleep` to hold execution after a right-click.

Get the Number of Elements Present on a Web Page

In Chapter 2, you fetched the count using the native JavaScript `.length` property. It was lengthy, and the promise had to be resolved using a `.then` method. Let's look at a simpler API provided by Protractor to do the same task.

First, reuse the following three lines of code from the last few Super Calculator examples.

```
element(by.model('first')).sendKeys('5');
element(by.model('second')).sendKeys('8');
element(by.id('gobutton')).click();
```

Wrap them in a function and name it `addFun`. There is one enhancement that can be done to the `addFun()` function. Instead of using hard-coded values of 5 and 8, let's generate random values using JavaScript's math library. `Math.random()` generates a random number between 0 and 1; for instance, 0.1101467.

When you multiply the generated random number to 100, you get a random number between 1 and 100. Since the result is not a whole number, you apply `Math.floor()` to the entire result, which returns the largest integer less than or equal to its input number, meaning it removes all the fraction digits in the output. The optimized `addFun()` should look like the following.

```
function addFun() {
    const num1 = Math.floor((Math.random() * 100));
    const num2 = Math.floor((Math.random() * 100));
```

```
    element(by.model('first')).sendKeys(`${num1}`);
    element(by.model('second')).sendKeys(`${num2}`);
    element(by.id('gobutton')).click();
}
```

Note that async/await is not used in the function because none of the code is dependent on a server response. Also, if you want to learn more about `${num1}` syntax, refer to the information on template literals at https://developer.mozilla.org/en-US/docs/Web/JavaScript/Reference/Template_literals.

https://developer.mozilla.org/en-US/docs/Web/JavaScript/Reference/Template_literals

In Listing 4-10 uses the addFun() function a few times on the web page and counts the number of resulting rows.

Listing 4-10.   Count of Repeated Elements

```
it('Should count the number of rows after multiple add operations',
async function () {
    await browser.get('http://juliemr.github.io/protractor-demo/');
    addFun();
    addFun();
    addFun();
    console.log("Count is: ")
    console.log(await element.all(by.repeater("result in memory")).
    count());
})
```

Output

Figure 4-13 shows that the count registered in the console terminal is 3, which is in line with the number of times you performed the action on the web page in Figure 4-10. Try to add await in front of addFun() anyway to see if Visual Studio Code gives any cue in response to your action.

```
PS F:\AUTOMATION\Protractor> protractor conf.js
[14:23:15] I/launcher - Running 1 instances of WebDriver
[14:23:15] I/hosted - Using the selenium server at http://localhost:4444/wd/hub
Started
************************Count is:
3
```

Figure 4-13. *Count of repeated result rows*

Get the First Element Returned from an Array of Elements

You see how to identify the first element uniquely upon receiving an array of multiple elements and then fetch its text. Listing 4-11 modifies Listing 4-10.

Syntax

```
element.all(by.locator("value")).first()
```

Listing 4-11. Getting Text of the First Element Fetched from Repeating Rows

```
it('Should fetch text of First element from result rows', async function () {
    await browser.get('http://juliemr.github.io/protractor-demo/');
    addFun();
    addFun();
    addFun();
    await browser.sleep(5000)
    console.log("First result is: ")
    console.log(await element.all(by.repeater("result in memory")).first().
    getText());
})
```

Output

In Figure 4-14, the first row of the repeater in the result section matches the console output. Since `Math.random()` is used, the resulting text in your machine does not match mine. The pass criteria for the test is that, at your end, it should also fetch the first result row successfully in the console terminal.

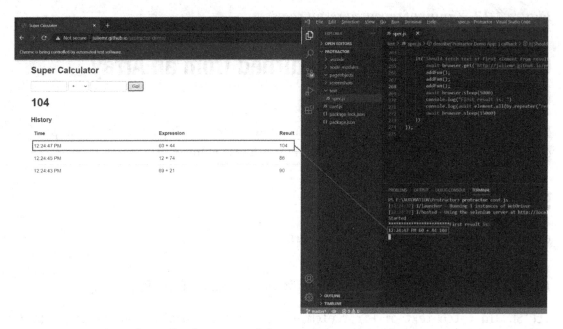

Figure 4-14. *Text from the first row of the result repeater elements*

Notes

Note the following line from Figure 4-1.

```
console.log(await element.all(by.repeater("result in memory")).first().
getText());
```

It can be broken into three lines for more flexibility, as follows.

```
var first_elem= await element.all(by.repeater("result in memory")).first();
var first_elem_text= await first_elem.getText()
console.log(first_elem_text);
```

EXERCISE

Try to fetch the text of the last element in the results after execution using `.last()`.

Get Any Element Returned from an Array of Elements

If you want to get any element other than the first and last, use Protractor's `.get()` API, which uses an index. `.get(0)` fetches the first element in Figure 4-15 and `.get(1)` fetches the second element. Let's fetch the second element in Listing 4-12 using the same example in the past two demonstrations.

Syntax

```
element.all(by.locator("value")).get(n)
```

Listing 4-12. Getting Text of the Second Element Fetched from Repeating Rows

```
it('Should fetch text of Second element from result rows', async
function () {
    await browser.get('http://juliemr.github.io/protractor-demo/');
    addFun();
    addFun();
    addFun();
    await browser.sleep(5000);
    console.log("Second result is: ");
    var second_elem = await element.all(by.repeater("result in memory")).
    get(1);
    var second_elem_text = await second_elem.getText()
    console.log(second_elem_text);
})
```

Output

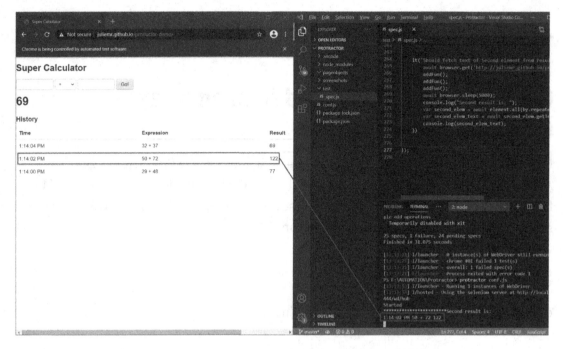

Figure 4-15. *Text from the second row of the result repeater elements*

Iterate All Elements

There are many instances where you want to iterate through all the elements fetched by your locator; for example, clicking multiple links or getting the text of multiple elements. Let's again edit the code in Figure 4-13 and learn how to get the text of all the identified by iterating them using the .each method in Protractor.

Syntax

```
element.all(by.locator("value")).each(function () { });
```

Listing 4-13. Iterating All Result Elements Fetched and Printing Their Text

```
it('Should fetch text of all result element rows', async function () {
    await browser.get('http://juliemr.github.io/protractor-demo/');
    addFun();
```

```
    addFun();
    addFun();
    await browser.sleep(5000);
    console.log("All result rows: ");
    var result_elems = await element.all(by.repeater("result in memory"));
    result_elems.each(async function (item) {
        console.log(await item.getText());
    });
    await browser.sleep(15000);

})
```

Output

Figure 4-16 shows that Protractor's `.each` API is similar to the `.forEach` method in JavaScript. The `console.log` statement is individually applied to all the elements fetched in the array by `element.all`.

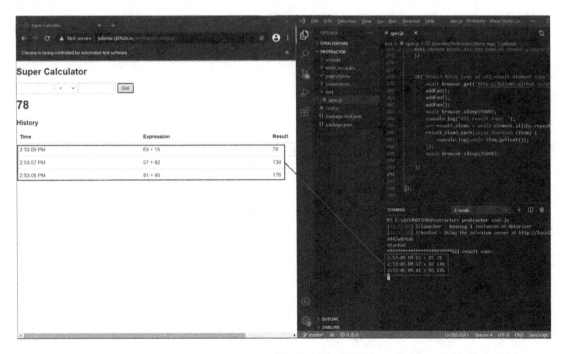

Figure 4-16. *Iterated through all the elements fetched by element.all and printed result of all repeater elements*

Notes

You are more likely to get a list of elements retrieved by selectors such as `className` and `tagName`, or a CSS selector rather than name and ID, which usually only fetch a unique element.

Summary

Along with learning some basics, you learned how to automate simple browser user actions. You continue this journey in the next chapter, where you learn Protractor's way of automating user actions.

CHAPTER 5

Web Page Interactions II

In the last chapter, you learned about automating a few basic user actions on a web page. Let's continue the journey and learn some more user actions with the help of Protractor API. You about learn the following.

- Testing a non-Angular application

- Getting a processed config file

- Getting a web page source

- Getting a web page title and URL

- Refreshing a web page and restart browser

- Navigating back and forward

- Maximizing the browser

- Getting and setting the window size and position

- Getting an element location

- Opening and closing a new tab

- Scrolling to an element

Testing non-Angular Web Pages

Protractor is customized specifically to work best on Angular applications. There are instances in an Angular web app, however, where some components or web pages are non-Angular. Protractor is required to automate user actions on a non-Angular web app. You can determine if a web page is built with Angular by going into the Chrome developer console **(Ctrl+Shift+I)**, typing **window.angular**, and hitting Enter. `window.angular` is the global `angular.js` variable that is created once AngularJS has been fully

© Shashank Shukla 2021
S. Shukla, *The Protractor Handbook*, https://doi.org/10.1007/978-1-4842-7289-3_5

loaded from a `script` tag. Protractor uses the APIs exposed by the Angular framework—like `$timeout` and `$http`—to synchronize the page created by Angular's asynchronous components. If the page does not have Angular components, it returns undefined because Protractor is trying to synchronize the page using the `window.angular` API, which is not available on the page.

Figure 5-1 compares `protractor.org`, a known Angular web page, to `internet.heroku.com`, a known non-Angular web page.

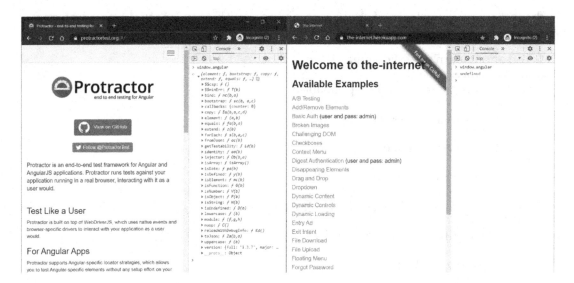

Figure 5-1. *Comparing window.angular result for an Angular and non-Angular site*

Let's automate the user functions on this non-Angular web site. Protractor provides a method called `browser.waitForAngularEnabled()`, which is set to `true` by default. If it is set to `false` before launching any Protractor-provided browser commands, Protractor starts interacting with the browser without waiting for Angular `$http` and `$timeout` calls to complete, assuming it is not interacting with a web page built with Angular.

Syntax

```
browser.waitForAngularEnabled(false)
```

Listing 5-1. Placing waitForAngular(false) Before Testing internet.heroku.com

```
it('Should test non-angular web page', async function () {
    browser.waitForAngularEnabled(false)
    await browser.get('https://the-internet.herokuapp.com/');
    browser.takeScreenshot().then(function (element) {
        let stream = fs.createWriteStream('./screenshots/heroku.png');
        stream.write(new Buffer.from(element, 'base64'));
        stream.end();
    })
})
```

Output

Figure 5-2 shows the screenshot successfully captured by Protractor on a non-Angular web page.

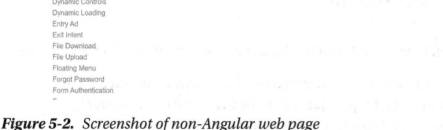

Figure 5-2. *Screenshot of non-Angular web page*

Notes

`waitForAngular()` method can be toggled true or false as a switch multiple times in the same test case if the user transitions between Angular and non-Angular pages in a web app. During the execution, you can see the state of the switch by using `console.log(await browser.waitForAngularEnabled());`. Toggling the switch can be confusing, and it becomes applicable to the entire driver session if it is not toggled back. Hence, Protractor recommends using the wrapped `driver` tag directly rather than toggling the `waitForAngularEnabled` property.

In Table 5-1, if you omit `waitForAngularEnabled` and use `browser.driver.get` and `browser.driver.takeScreenshot`, the code can still successfully test the non-Angular web page.

Table 5-1.

Method Call	Usage
`browser.get`	Used when the web page has Angular components
`browser.driver.get`	Used when the web page doesn't have Angular components

Get the Processed Configuration File

You can fetch the values of the processed configuration file using the syntax shown in Listing 5-2.

Syntax

`browser.getProcessedConfig());`

Listing 5-2. Fetching the Value of the Input Field and Printing It in the Console

```
it('Should fetch processed configuration file', async function () {
    await browser.get('http://juliemr.github.io/protractor-demo/');
    console.log(await browser.getProcessedConfig());
})
```

Output

Figure 5-3 shows the console output, which can be validated against the `conf.js` file in the framework.

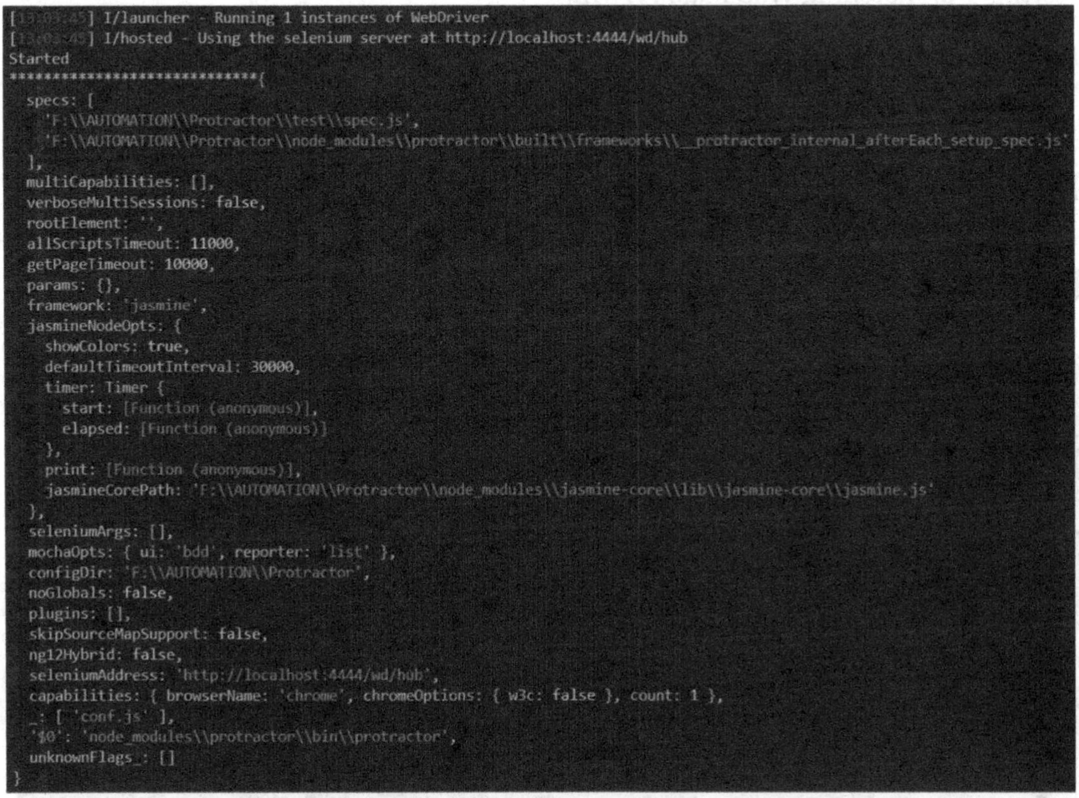

```
[13:03:45] I/launcher - Running 1 instances of WebDriver
[13:03:45] I/hosted - Using the selenium server at http://localhost:4444/wd/hub
Started
*****************************{
  specs: [
    'F:\\AUTOMATION\\Protractor\\test\\spec.js',
    'F:\\AUTOMATION\\Protractor\\node_modules\\protractor\\built\\frameworks\\__protractor_internal_afterEach_setup_spec.js'
  ],
  multiCapabilities: [],
  verboseMultiSessions: false,
  rootElement: '',
  allScriptsTimeout: 11000,
  getPageTimeout: 10000,
  params: {},
  framework: 'jasmine',
  jasmineNodeOpts: {
    showColors: true,
    defaultTimeoutInterval: 30000,
    timer: Timer {
      start: [Function (anonymous)],
      elapsed: [Function (anonymous)]
    },
    print: [Function (anonymous)],
    jasmineCorePath: 'F:\\AUTOMATION\\Protractor\\node_modules\\jasmine-core\\lib\\jasmine-core\\jasmine.js'
  },
  seleniumArgs: [],
  mochaOpts: { ui: 'bdd', reporter: 'list' },
  configDir: 'F:\\AUTOMATION\\Protractor',
  noGlobals: false,
  plugins: [],
  skipSourceMapSupport: false,
  ng12Hybrid: false,
  seleniumAddress: 'http://localhost:4444/wd/hub',
  capabilities: { browserName: 'chrome', chromeOptions: { w3c: false }, count: 1 },
  _: [ 'conf.js' ],
  '$0': 'node_modules\\protractor\\bin\\protractor',
  unknownFlags_: []
}
```

Figure 5-3. *Screenshot of processed conf.js configuration file*

Get a Web Page Source Code File

A web page's source code can be printed in the console terminal using the syntax shown in Listing 5-3. If a web page is modified with JavaScript after loading, this command may return the page source before modification took place. Usually, this command verifies if a specific text is present on a page (even if it's hidden in UI) and decides whether to proceed or not.

Syntax

```
browser.getPageSource();
```

Listing 5-3.   Fetching Web Page HTML

```
it('Should fetch web page\'s source code', async function () {
    await browser.get('http://juliemr.github.io/protractor-demo/');
    console.log(await browser.getPageSource());
})
```

Output

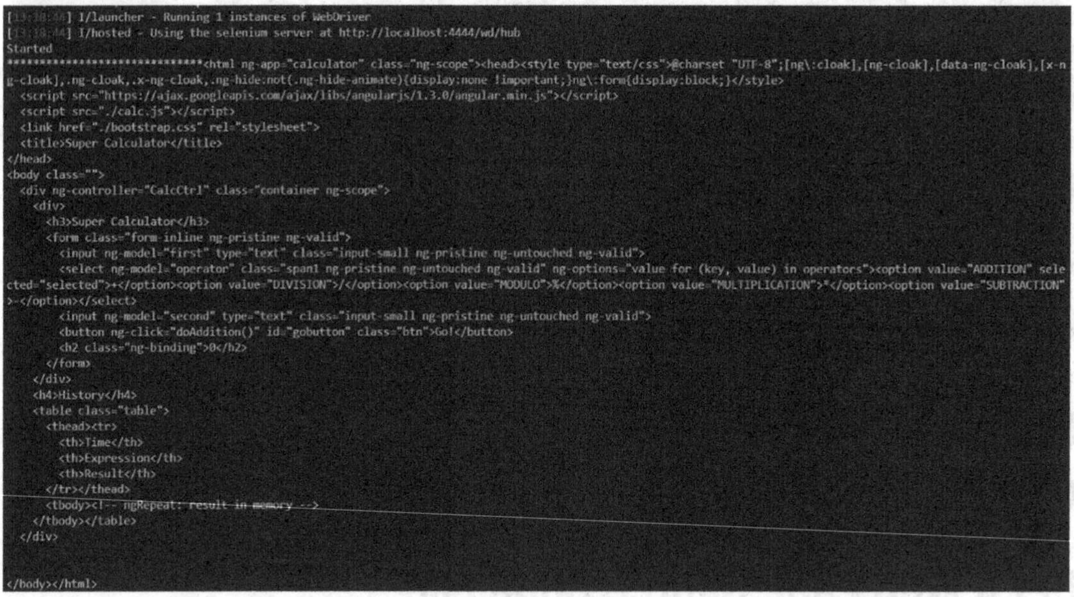

Figure 5-4.   *Screenshot of Super Calculator web page's HTML source code*

Get a Web Page Title and URL

You often need to validate the web page's title or URL against the test script to ensure that you are navigating to the correct page or URL. The following syntax is very helpful in making those assertions, as shown in Listing 5-4.

Syntax

```
browser.getTitle();
browser.getCurrentUrl();
```

Listing 5-4. Fetching Web Page HTML

```
it('Should fetch web page\'s title & URL', async function () {
    await browser.get('http://juliemr.github.io/protractor-demo/');
    console.log("Title:- " + await browser.getTitle());
    console.log("URL:- " + await browser.getCurrentUrl());
})
```

Output

Figure 5-5 shows the title and the URL of the Super Calculator web page printed in the console terminal.

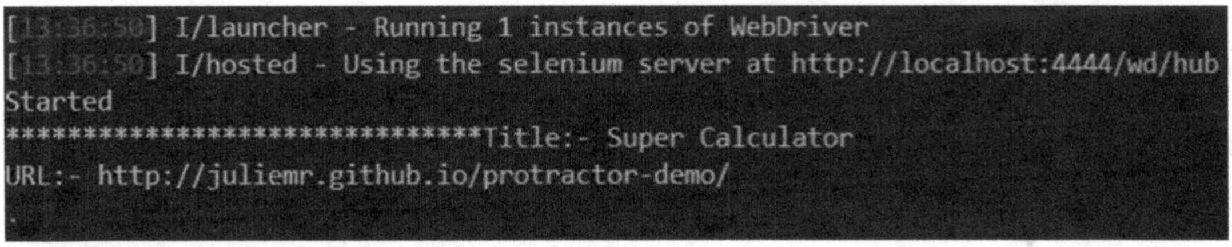

```
[13:36:50] I/launcher - Running 1 instances of WebDriver
[13:36:50] I/hosted - Using the selenium server at http://localhost:4444/wd/hub
Started
*******************************Title:- Super Calculator
URL:- http://juliemr.github.io/protractor-demo/
```

Figure 5-5. *Title and URL of the web page*

Refreshing a Web Page

You can refresh a web page with the syntax available in the WebDriverJS Navigate class used by Protractor, as shown in Listing 5-5. Refreshing fully reloads the current page, assuming the page being loaded uses Angular. If you need to refresh a page that does not have Angular on load, use the wrapped web driver directly.

Syntax

```
browser.refresh()
```

Listing 5-5. Refreshing the Web Page

```
it('Should refresh the web page', async function () {
    await browser.get('http://juliemr.github.io/protractor-demo/');
    addFun();
    await browser.sleep(4000)
    await browser.refresh();
    await browser.sleep(4000)
})
```

Output

You see a visible difference in the web page's content before and after the refresh since the input has been erased. To observe this, set your preferred breakpoints and run the test in Debug mode.

Notes

Alternatively, you can also refresh a page by using an F5 key press in any input field on a page as `await element(by.model('first')).sendKeys(protractor.Key.F5);`. Keep in mind that when you interact with an element and refresh the page, the element becomes stale because it is destroyed and then reconstructed. You get the following error.

`Stale Element Reference Exception`

The following is an excerpt from the official Selenium web site (`www.selenium.dev`).

The most frequent cause of Stale Element Reference Exception is that page that the element was part of has been refreshed, or the user has navigated away to another page. A less common but still common cause is where a JS library has deleted an element and replaced it with one with the same ID or attributes.

It should be used only where there is a strong need for refreshing the application web page being tested. To avoid an error, save the element's locator strategy in a JavaScript variable and use it again after the page is refreshed. This approach allows a fresh element value via the locator after the DOM is reloaded.

Navigating to a New URL in a Browser

The command in Figure 5-6 navigates to a URL.

Syntax

```
browser.navigate().to('url')
```

Listing 5-6. Browser Navigating to /api'

```
it('Should navigate to web page', async function () {
    await browser.get('https://www.protractortest.org/#/');
    console.log("Webpage 1: " + await browser.getCurrentUrl())
    await browser.navigate().to('https://www.protractortest.org/#/api')
    console.log("Webpage 2: " + await browser.getCurrentUrl())
})
```

Output

```
[16:41:47] I/launcher - Running 1 instances of WebDriver
[16:41:47] I/hosted - Using the selenium server at http://localhost:4444/wd/hub
Started
*********************************Webpage 1: https://www.protractortest.org/#/
Webpage 2: https://www.protractortest.org/#/api
.
```

Figure 5-6. *Navigating from Protractor Homepage to Protractor API reference page*

Notes

You may have noticed that `browser.get('url')` and `browser.navigate().to('url')` methods were used in the same example. You might be wondering if these methods are interchangeable, but there is a subtle difference between the two APIs. The `browser.get('url')` method opens a URL and automatically waits until the whole page is loaded before returning control to the test or script. For single-page applications, the difference between these two methods becomes a little more prominent in terms of how the application works and how browsers deal with it. `browser.navigate().to('url')` navigates to the page by changing the URL, like forward/backward navigation; whereas, `browser.get('url')` refreshes the page, thereby changing the URL. Refer to `https://w3c.github.io/webdriver/#dfn-navigate-to` for more information.

In cases where the web app's domain changes, both methods behave similarly; that is, the page is refreshed in both cases. But, in single-page applications, while `browser.navigate().to('url')` does not refresh the page, `browser.get('url')` does.

Go to `https://en.wikipedia.org/wiki/Single-page_application` for more information.

Navigating Back in a Browser

This command navigates backward, as shown in Listing 5-7.

Syntax

`browser.navigate().back()`

Listing 5-7. Browser Navigating Backward

```
it('Should navigate back to visited web page', async function () {
    await browser.get('https://www.protractortest.org/#/');
    console.log("Webpage 1: " + await browser.getCurrentUrl())
    await browser.navigate().to('https://www.protractortest.org/#/api')
    console.log("Webpage 2: " + await browser.getCurrentUrl())
    await browser.navigate().back()
    console.log("Webpage 1: " + await browser.getCurrentUrl())
})
```

Output

As you can see in Figure 5-7, the user navigates to the Protractor API reference page and then back to Protractor's home page. For the sake of clarity, the previous `it` blocks, which are not in use, are moved to another file (named `archive.txt`) under the `test` folder.

```
[22:30:22] I/launcher - Running 1 instances of WebDriver
[22:30:22] I/hosted - Using the selenium server at http://localhost:4444/wd/hub
Started
Webpage 1: https://www.protractortest.org/#/
Webpage 2: https://www.protractortest.org/#/api
Webpage 1: https://www.protractortest.org/#/
```

Figure 5-7. *Navigating from Protractor homepage to Protractor API reference page and back*

Navigating Forward in a Browser

As shown in Listing 5-8, this command is used to navigate forward.

Syntax

```
browser.forward()
```

Listing 5-8. Browser Navigating Forward

```
it('Should navigate forward to visited web page', async function () {
    await browser.get('https://www.protractortest.org/#/');
    console.log("Webpage 1: " + await browser.getCurrentUrl())
    await browser.navigate().to('https://www.protractortest.org/#/api')
    console.log("Webpage 2: " + await browser.getCurrentUrl())
    await browser.navigate().back()
    console.log("Webpage 1: " + await browser.getCurrentUrl())
    await browser.navigate().forward()
    console.log("Webpage 2: " + await browser.getCurrentUrl())
})
```

Output

```
[22:50:24] I/launcher - Running 1 instances of WebDriver
[22:50:24] I/hosted - Using the selenium server at http://localhost:4444/wd/hub
Started
Webpage 1: https://www.protractortest.org/#/
Webpage 2: https://www.protractortest.org/#/api
Webpage 1: https://www.protractortest.org/#/
Webpage 2: https://www.protractortest.org/#/api
.
```

Figure 5-8. *Navigating back and forth between Protractor homepage and Protractor API reference page*

Maximizing the Browser

browser.manage().window().maximize() command maximizes the browser according to your screen dimensions. If your browser is not maximized before the Protractor framework starts locating the elements, there is a chance that all the elements on the web application may not be visible, resulting in test failure because the element must be visible within the viewport for it to be interactive in Selenium. It's also easier to view web pages and take screenshots on maximized browser windows. Listing 5-9 shows how to maximize your browser before the start of the test.

Syntax

```
browser.manage().window().maximize();
```

Listing 5-9. Maximizing the Window

```
it('Should maximize the browser window', async function () {
    await browser.get('https://www.protractortest.org/#/');
    await browser.manage().window().maximize();
    await browser.sleep(3000)
})
```

Output

There is no output present in the console, but you need to be observant of the browser behavior while the test is being executed to ensure that the outcome is expected. The browser should launch and be maximized, and then stay maximized for 3 seconds before closing.

Notes

The best practice is to place this function right after the `browser.get()` command in your test script so the element's possibility of coming into the viewport—and therefore being located—increases considerably.

Getting and Setting Window Size and Position

Sometimes you must test your web application in a specific window size to see how the elements are rendered and whether there is any discrepancy that can be caught while using the web app on a specifically sized window on a tablet or a mobile phone. You can use the syntax shown in Listing 5-10 to set the browser's specific window size and position.

Syntax

```
browser.driver.manage().window().setPosition(x, y);
browser.driver.manage().window().setSize(width, height);
```

Listing 5-10. Get Browser Window Position and Size

```
    it('Should set position & size of the browser window', async function () {
        await browser.get('https://www.protractortest.org/#/');
//   x & y set the position of the screen.
        let x = 100;
        let y = 100;
// width & height set size of the screen
        let width = 800;
        let height = 600;
```

```
        await browser.driver.manage().window().setPosition(x, y);
        await browser.driver.manage().window().setSize(width, height);
        await browser.sleep(3000);
    })
```

Output

With the help of manual intervention (print screen), Figure 5-9 shows how the browser window looks.

Figure 5-9. *Browser window with user-specified size and position parameters*

EXERCISE

Try to change the x, y, width, and height parameters in Listing 5-10 and observe how the parameters affect the browser window's position and size.

Getting Element Location and Size

If you need to get the location and size of the element for validation, you can use the methods shown in Listing 5-11.

Syntax

```
element(by.locator('value')).getLocation()
element(by.locator('value')).getSize()
```

Listing 5-11. Get Element Location and Size

```
it('Should get position & size of an element', async function () {
    await browser.get('https://www.protractortest.org/#/');
    let logo_location = await element(by.className('protractor-logo')).
    getLocation()
    let logo_size = await element(by.className('protractor-logo')).
    getSize()
    console.log("Logo Location is: ")
    console.log(logo_location)
    console.log("Logo Size is: ")
    console.log(logo_size)
})
```

Output

Figure 5-10 shows the position and size of the element. The value in the variables `logo_position` and `logo_size` are objects with x, y, width, or height as one of their properties. Properties are accessed using the dot operator (i.e., `object.property` or `object['property']`). While implementing the test case in your test suite, bear in mind that the size and position are relative to the browser. If you change the size of the browser (see Listing 5-10) before fetching the size and position, you will get different values. This means that if the same test script is run on a different display resolution or monitor size, the output of `getSize()` and `getLocation()` method may differ.

```
[12:19:26] I/launcher - Running 1 instances of WebDriver
[12:19:26] I/hosted - Using the selenium server at http://localhost:4444/wd/hub
Started
Logo Location is:
{
  ceil: {},
  clone: {},
  floor: {},
  round: {},
  scale: {},
  translate: {},
  x: 285.9756164550781,
  y: 89.98983764648438
}
Logo Size is:
{
  aspectRatio: {},
  ceil: {},
  clone: {},
  floor: {},
  height: 101,
  round: {},
  scale: {},
  width: 450
}
```

Figure 5-10. *Protractor logo's position and size*

EXERCISE

In Listing 5-11, fetch the specific x, y, width, and height properties for the logo. position and logo.size objects, respectively, in the console terminal.

Open a New Tab

Open a new tab in the browser, as shown in Listing 5-12.

Syntax

```
browser.executeScript(window.open())
```

Listing 5-12. Opens a New Tab in the Same Browser

```
    it('Should open a new tab in the same browser window', async function
() {
        await browser.get('https://www.protractortest.org/#/');
        browser.executeScript('window.open("http://juliemr.github.io/
        protractor-demo/")')
        await browser.sleep(4000)
    })
```

Output

Figure 5-11 shows that a new tab with a specific URL is opened in the browser.

Figure 5-11. *A new tab is opened in the same window*

Close a New Tab

Close a tab in the browser, as shown in Listing 5-13.

Syntax

```
await browser.close()
```

Listing 5-13. Open a New Tab in the Same Browser

```
it('Should close the browser window', async function () {
    await browser.get('https://www.protractortest.org/#/');
    await browser.sleep(5000)
    await browser.close()
})
```

Output

The browser closes after 5 seconds. If you want to restart the browser, you can use `await browser.restart();` instead. Be advised that a new session ID is assigned to the browser after restart.

Scroll to an Element

This method allows the control to scroll to an element's location. Since there is no custom Protractor API for this, `browser.execute` achieves the scrolling, as shown in Listing 5-14.

Syntax

Listing 5-14. Scroll to an Element

```
it('Should close the browser window', async function () {
    await browser.get('https://www.protractortest.org/#/');
    console.log(await browser.getCurrentUrl());
    await browser.executeScript('window.scrollTo(0, document.body.
    scrollHeight);').then(function () {
        element(by.linkText("Tutorial")).click();
    })
    console.log(await browser.getCurrentUrl());
})
```

Output

The document.body.scrollHeight parameter denotes the total height of the web page, which means scroll to the bottom of the page where the tutorial element is located and click it.

```
[09:51:08] I/launcher - 0 instance(s) of WebDriver still running
[09:51:08] I/launcher - chrome #01 passed
PS F:\AUTOMATION\Protractor> protractor conf.js
[09:51:29] I/launcher - Running 1 instances of WebDriver
[09:51:29] I/hosted - Using the selenium server at http://localhost:4444/wd/hub
Started
https://www.protractortest.org/#/
https://www.protractortest.org/#/tutorial
.


1 spec, 0 failures
Finished in 10.849 seconds
```

Figure 5-12. *URL tutorial clicked and navigated*

Summary

After trying out these examples, I am sure you will be much more confident in your understanding of the workings and capabilities of the Protractor tool. There are thousands of possibilities when you automate an end-to-end flow, but once you know the fundamentals, you can start exploring and experimenting with different browser commands and build upon your existing knowledge to automate even the most complex tests. Now that you have learned about installation, locators, and some simple APIs, the next chapters look at some complex Protractor for web page interaction.

CHAPTER 6

Web Page Interactions III

This chapter wraps up all the remaining Protractor APIs that perform respective user actions. You will learn the following:

- Uploading a file and submitting a form

- Getting the location of an element

- Handling drop-downs

- Dragging and dropping

- Mouse-hovering actions

- Executing scripts

- Switching between frames and tabs

- Handling alerts

- Getting an element's ID, attribute, tag name, and CSS property

Uploading a File

There are scenarios where you need to upload a file on a web page, as shown in Figure 6-1. Protractor provides no separate API to upload a file, so make sure that the field is an `input` type HTML tag. Then, the `sendKeys` command provides the absolute path of the file for the Upload button, as done in Listing 6-1.

© Shashank Shukla 2021
S. Shukla, *The Protractor Handbook*, https://doi.org/10.1007/978-1-4842-7289-3_6

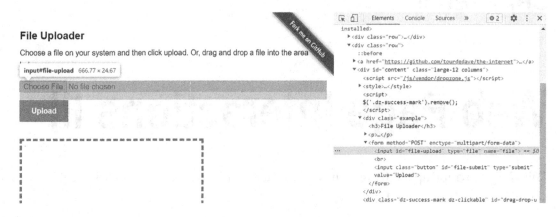

Figure 6-1. *Choose the file element of input tag type*

Syntax

```
element(by.<locator>('Input tag's locator')).sendKeys('<Path to file
in local disk>');
```

Listing 6-1. Uploading File from Local Disk to Web Page

```
it('Should verify file uploaded successfully, async function () {
    browser.waitForAngularEnabled(false)
    await browser.get('https://the-internet.herokuapp.com/upload');
    await element(by.id('file-upload')).sendKeys('F:\\Untitled.png');
    await element(by.id('file-submit')).click()
    await browser.takeScreenshot().then(function (element) {
        let stream = fs.createWriteStream('./screenshots/
        fileuploadmsg.png');
        stream.write(new Buffer.from(element, 'base64'));
        stream.end();
    })
})
```

Output

Figure 6-2 is a screenshot of the success message after the file successfully uploads.

Figure 6-2. *File upload success message on web page*

Notes

The absolute path of the file should be the actual file location on your local disk.

Submitting a Form

If a form on the web page doesn't have a Submit button, use `.sendKeys(protractor.Key.ENTER);`, which sends the Enter key on the `input` tag, thereby submitting your form.

Getting the Location of an Element on a Web Page

The element's location can be found using the `getLocation` API provided by Protractor, as shown in Listing 6-3. The location is not absolute, however, meaning it is relative to the browser window. If the browser is maximized, it also changes according to screen size.

Syntax

```
element(by.id('locator')).getLocation()
```

Listing 6-2. Fetching Location Coordinates of Web Elements

```
it('Should get location of an element', async function () {
    await browser.get('http://juliemr.github.io/protractor-demo/');
    await element(by.id('gobutton')).getLocation().then(function (item) {
        console.log('coordinates are:');
        console.log(item);
    })
```

101

Output

Figure 6-3 shows the coordinates of the element with respect to the browser size. If the x and y coordinates are required for validation, the values can be obtained separately as well by replacing `console.log(item);` to `console.log(item.x);` for the x axis and `console.log(item.y);` for the y axis.

```
PS F:\AUTOMATION\Protractor> protractor conf.js
[08:32:49] I/launcher - Running 1 instances of WebDriver
[08:32:49] I/hosted - Using the selenium server at http://localhost:4444/wd/hub
Started
Cordinates are:
{
  ceil: {},
  clone: {},
  floor: {},
  round: {},
  scale: {},
  translate: {},
  x: 328.7347412109375,
  y: 60.09908676147461
}


1 spec, 0 failures
Finished in 2.091 seconds
```

Figure 6-3. *Output received in coordinates*

EXERCISE

Maximize the browser before navigating to the URL in Listing 6-2. Observe the difference in output when the browser is opened in a window compared to when it is maximized.

Handling Drop-Downs

Drop-downs allow the user to choose one value from a predefined list. It displays a list of options from which the user can select one (see Figure 6-4). User actions on a drop-down can be automated in three ways.

- Selecting an option by its attribute value

- Selecting an option by its index

- Selecting an option by its visible text

Let's relook at addFun() from Chapter 4, as shown in Listing 6-3.

Listing 6-3. Addition Function for Super Calculator Web Page

```
function addFun() {
    const num1 = Math.floor((Math.random() * 100));
    const num2 = Math.floor((Math.random() * 100));
    element(by.model('first')).sendKeys(`${num1}`);
    element(by.model('second')).sendKeys(`${num2}`);
    element(by.id('gobutton')).click();
}
```

Listing 6-3 has not factored the selection of the operator because the + operator is selected by default. This is not a very robust approach, but it works as a temporary measure. As shown in Figure 6-4, four other operators need to be factored into the drop-down.

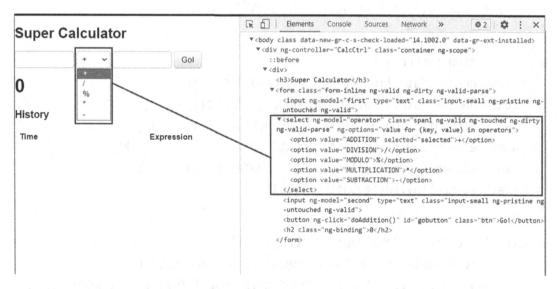

Figure 6-4. *Other operators available in the drop-down*

Listing 6-4 creates a function that subtracts the given numbers and provides the output in the console. The function is similar to addFun with one addition—locating the operator in the drop-down and clicking it using the command provided in the syntax. Let's call it subFun().

Syntax

```
element(by.cssContainingText('<attribute>', '<text>')).click()
```

Listing 6-4. Selecting the - Operator from Drop-Down

```
const { Buffer } = require('buffer');
var fs = require('fs');
const { browser, element } = require('protractor');

async function addFun() {
    const num1 = Math.floor((Math.random() * 100));
    const num2 = Math.floor((Math.random() * 100));
    await element(by.model('first')).sendKeys(`${num1}`);
    await element(by.model('second')).sendKeys(`${num2}`);
    await element(by.id('gobutton')).click();
}

async function subFun() {
    const num1 = Math.floor((Math.random() * 100));
    const num2 = Math.floor((Math.random() * 100));
    await element(by.model('first')).sendKeys(`${num1}`);
    await element(by.cssContainingText('option', '-')).click();
    await element(by.model('second')).sendKeys(`${num2}`);
    await element(by.id('gobutton')).click();
}

describe('Protractor Demo App: ', function () {
    it('Should subtract the two numbers', async function () {
        await browser.get('http://juliemr.github.io/protractor-demo/');
        await subFun();
```

```
await element(by.tagName('body')).takeScreenshot().then(function
(element) {
    let stream = fs.createWriteStream('./screenshots/subtract.png');
    stream.write(new Buffer.from(element, 'base64'));
    stream.end();
    })
  })
});
```

Output

Figure 6-5 is a screenshot capturing the body tag. It shows the subtraction of two random numbers.

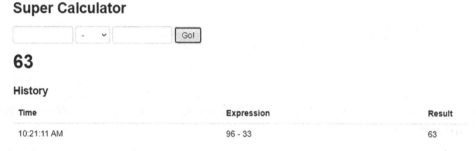

Figure 6-5. *Title and URL of the web page*

EXERCISE

Try to add a step that selects the addition operator in the addFun() function, even though it is selected already, to make it more foolproof for future changes on the web page.

You can also group all the operators into one function where you pass three parameters—num1, num2, and operator—and use the if else method to determine what operation to perform based on the value of the operator.

Dragging and Dropping

Dragging and dropping can look complex, but with the help of Protractor, you only need a source locator and a target locator—and you are almost there. Figure 6-6 shows an ideal scenario that tests the drag-and-drop API. The AngularJS - Drag Me button can be dragged and dropped into the "Drop below:" box.

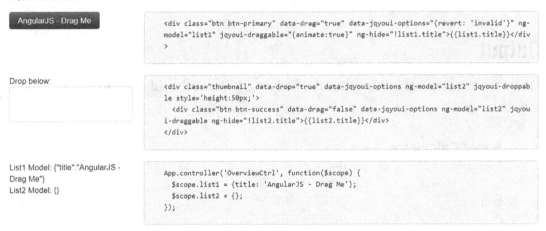

Figure 6-6. https://codef0rmer.github.io/angular-dragdrop/ drag-and-drop example

Listing 6-5 drags an element and drops it into its target location.

Syntax

```
browser.actions().dragAndDrop(<source>, <target>).perform();browser.refresh()
```

Listing 6-5. Drag-and-Drop

```
it('Should drag and drop elements', async function () {
    await browser.get('https://codef0rmer.github.io/angular-dragdrop/');
    var point1 = await element.all(by.css('div[class="span3"]')).get(0);
    var point2 = await element.all(by.css('div[class="span3"]')).get(1);
    await browser.actions().dragAndDrop(point1, point2).perform();
```

```
await element(by.className('row show-grid ng-scope')).takeScreenshot().
then(function (element) {
    let stream = fs.createWriteStream('./screenshots/drag.png');
    stream.write(new Buffer.from(element, 'base64'));
    stream.end();
})
})
```

Output

Figure 6-7 shows the `<div>` element dragged and dropped inside the target element.

Figure 6-7. https://codef0rmer.github.io/angular-dragdrop/ drag-and-drop example

Hovering the Mouse over an Element

The hover state refers to the properties of an element when you mouse over it. Hover properties, like a change of color or size, conveys the message that whatever the mouse is over can be interacted with. Consider Figure 6-8, where a user logged in to a web site named OrangeHRM, hovers over the Admin tab and then User Management to display the Users menu item, which redirects to the section containing all the user information in this demo web site.

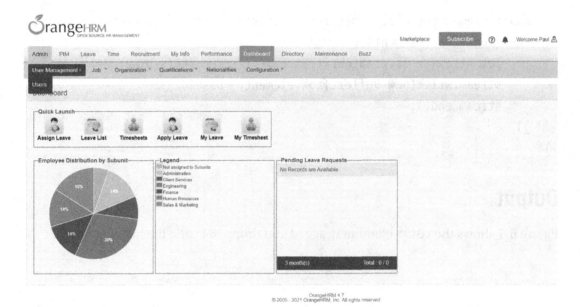

Figure 6-8. *https://opensource-demo.orangehrmlive.com/ mouse hover menu items*

In Listing 6-6, the user first sets the web page setting to non-Angular. It then navigates to OrangeHRM's login page, provides the default username and password, and navigates to the demo user's homepage. The user then hovers over the Users menu item, clicks it, and takes the screenshot of the navigated web page.

Syntax

```
browser.actions().mouseMove(admin).mouseMove(item1).perform()
```

Listing 6-6. Mouse Hover Function

```
it('Mouse Hover action', async function () {
    await browser.waitForAngularEnabled(false);
    await browser.get('https://opensource-demo.orangehrmlive.com/');
    await browser.element(by.id("txtUsername")).sendKeys("Admin");
    await browser.element(by.id("txtPassword")).sendKeys("admin123")
    await browser.element(by.id("btnLogin")).click();
```

```
var admin = await element(by.id('menu_admin_viewAdminModule'));
var usermgnt = await element(by.id('menu_admin_UserManagement'));
var users = await element(by.id('menu_admin_viewSystemUsers'));
await browser.actions().mouseMove(admin).mouseMove(usermgnt).
mouseMove(users).click().perform();// if you just want to move mouse
and don't do anything don't write .click()
await browser.takeScreenshot().then(function (element) {
    let stream = fs.createWriteStream('./screenshots/hover.png');
    stream.write(new Buffer.from(element, 'base64'));
    stream.end();
})
await browser.close();
})
```

Output

Some of the APIs covered in the book are included in the MouseHover example to make it an end-to-end test. Figure 6-9 shows the app's active users after the User Management drop-down is clicked. If the requirement is to just hover over the menu item, .click() can be omitted, as shown in the syntax.

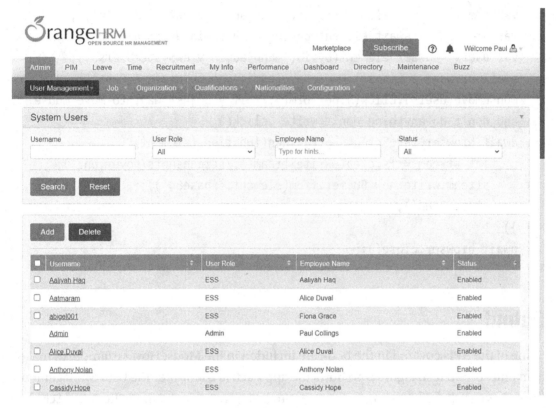

Figure 6-9. *List of users under Users menu item using the demo application*

The `Browser.actions()` class provides another way to perform drag-and-drop, which simulates the real-life user action of clicking a source element, moving it to the target element, and releasing it.

```
browser.actions()
    .mouseDown(element(by.<locator>('value')))
    .mouseMove(element(by.<locator>('value')))
    .mouseUp()
    .perform();
```

Execute Script

`browser.executeScript` command lets you run vanilla JavaScript on the web page. There are many use cases where you want to run JavaScript to achieve your objective during web automation. Listing 6-7 visits a non-Angular web site (`http://demo. automationtesting.in/Datepicker.html`), and the datepicker element is located and the date is selected.

Syntax

```
browser.forward()
```

Listing 6-7. Handling Datepicker

```
it('Datepicker demo', async function () {
    browser.waitForAngularEnabled(false);
    await browser.get('http://demo.automationtesting.in/Datepicker.html');
    await browser.executeScript("document.getElementById(
    'datepicker1').value='08/05/1989'")
    await browser.takeScreenshot().then(function (element) {
        let stream = fs.createWriteStream('./screenshots/datepicker.png');
        stream.write(new Buffer.from(element, 'base64'));
        stream.end();
    })
})
```

Output

Figure 6-10 shows the datepicker with the expected date.

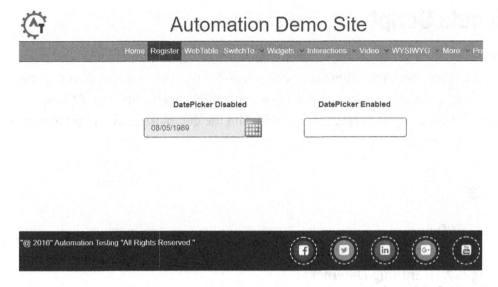

Figure 6-10. `http://demo.automationtesting.in/Datepicker.html` *handling a date picker*

Switching Between Windows

`browser.switchTo().window()` command helps you to switch browser windows (tabs). When a web page link opens in a new browser tab, you can use the command shown in Listing 6-8 to transfer control to the newly opened browser window and continue your test case automation journey. This example navigates to `http://demo.automationtesting.in/Windows.html` and clicks the button that opens a new browser tab (see Figure 6-11).

Figure 6-11.   *Click button to open a new window tab*

Syntax

```
browser.switchTo().window(<handle array index>)
```

Listing 6-8. Switching to Newly Opened Window

```
it('Window switch', async function () {
    await browser.waitForAngularEnabled(false)
    await browser.get('http://demo.automationtesting.in/Windows.html');
    await element(by.xpath("//*[@id='Tabbed']/a/button")).click();
    var handles = await browser.getAllWindowHandles();
    await browser.switchTo().window(handles[1]);
    await browser.takeScreenshot().then(function (element) {
        let stream = fs.createWriteStream('./screenshots/
        switchWindows.png');
        stream.write(new Buffer.from(element, 'base64'));
        stream.end();
    })
})
```

Output

Figure 6-12 shows the content of the newly opened tab. The captured screenshot shows a successful transfer of the control to the new tab.

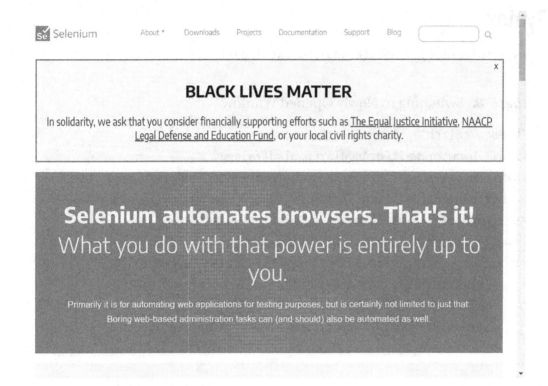

Figure 6-12. *Newly spawned tab*

Switching Between Frames Within a Web Page

Sometimes one web page is divided into many logical frames, where each frame can load its separate HTML document. Frames organize a page into different zones. An inline frame, or iFrame, is a part of HTML tags. It is a "box" that you can place anywhere on your web site to embed documents or the HTML body. Figure 6-13 shows the `www.selenium.dev/selenium/docs/api/java/index.html?overview-summary.html` web page, which is divided into three major frames.

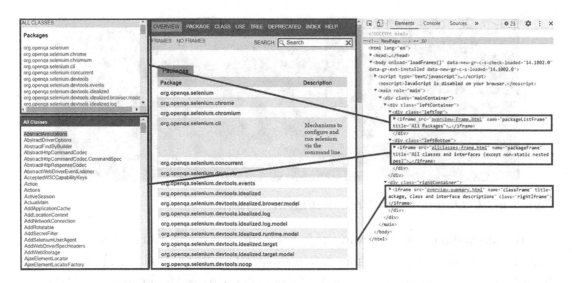

Figure 6-13. *Selenium.dev page layout*

Listing 6-9 shows switching to an iFrame to fetch the element with
AbstractAnnotations link text.

Listing 6-9. Switching to iFrame

```
it('Switching webpage frames', async function () {
    await browser.waitForAngularEnabled(false)
    await browser.get('https://www.selenium.dev/selenium/docs/api/java/
    index.html?overview-summary.html');
    await browser.sleep(1000);
    await browser.switchTo().frame("packageFrame");
    console.log("Element under All Classes:-")
    console.log(await browser.element(by.partialLinkText(
    'AbstractAnnotations')).getText());
    await browser.close()
})
```

Output

Figure 6-14 shows the output fetched from the frame.

```
PS F:\AUTOMATION\Protractor> protractor conf.js
[12:33:25] I/launcher - Running 1 instances of WebDriver
[12:33:25] I/hosted - Using the selenium server at http://localhost:4444/wd/hub
Started
Element under All Classes:-
AbstractAnnotations

.


1 spec, 0 failures
Finished in 7.225 seconds
```

Figure 6-14. *Output fetched from within the iFrame*

You cannot directly switch from one frame to another frame. You need to switch from the first frame to the main/parent frame using the `browser.switchTo().defaultContent()` command, and then from the main/parent frame to the second frame.

When there is a frame inside a frame, you need to go to the outer frame and then to its inner frame. In this scenario, you don't need to go to the main frame (i.e., parent frame) first.

EXERCISE

Listing 6-9 fetches another element's text from an iFrame different from `packageFrame`.

Alerts: Accepting an Alert

The `Alert()` method is used by developers to notify users about something important. It is displayed an alert pop-up box containing the intended message, an OK button, and sometimes a Cancel button, as shown in Figure 6-15.

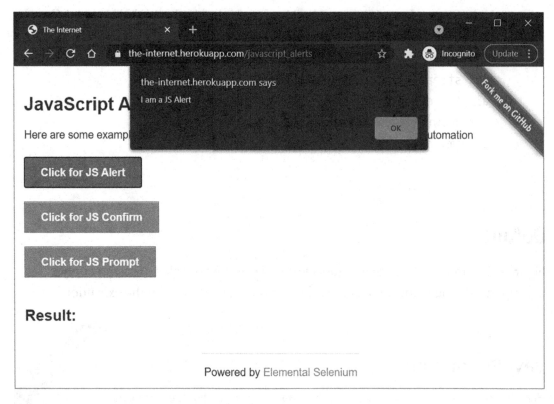

Figure 6-15. *Alert box with OK as an option*

The most common action required from the user is to accept the alert pop-up box by clicking the OK button (see Listing 6-10). When the alert box opens, it directs the user's focus from the rest of the web site, making it inaccessible, and forces the user to pay attention to the alert.

Syntax

```
browser.switchTo().alert().accept();
```

Listing 6-10. Accepting Alert

```
it('Handling alerts:Accept an alert', async function () {
    browser.waitForAngularEnabled(false);
    await browser.driver.get('https://the-internet.herokuapp.com/
    javascript_alerts');
```

```
await browser.element(by.css('button[onclick="jsAlert()"]')).click();
await browser.switchTo().alert().accept();
await browser.takeScreenshot().then(function (element) {
    let stream = fs.createWriteStream('./screenshots/
    alertaccept.png');
    stream.write(new Buffer.from(element, 'base64'));
    stream.end();
})
})
```

Output

Figure 6-16 captures the success message after accepting the alert. You can apply appropriate debug points or browser.sleep if you want to observe the execution.

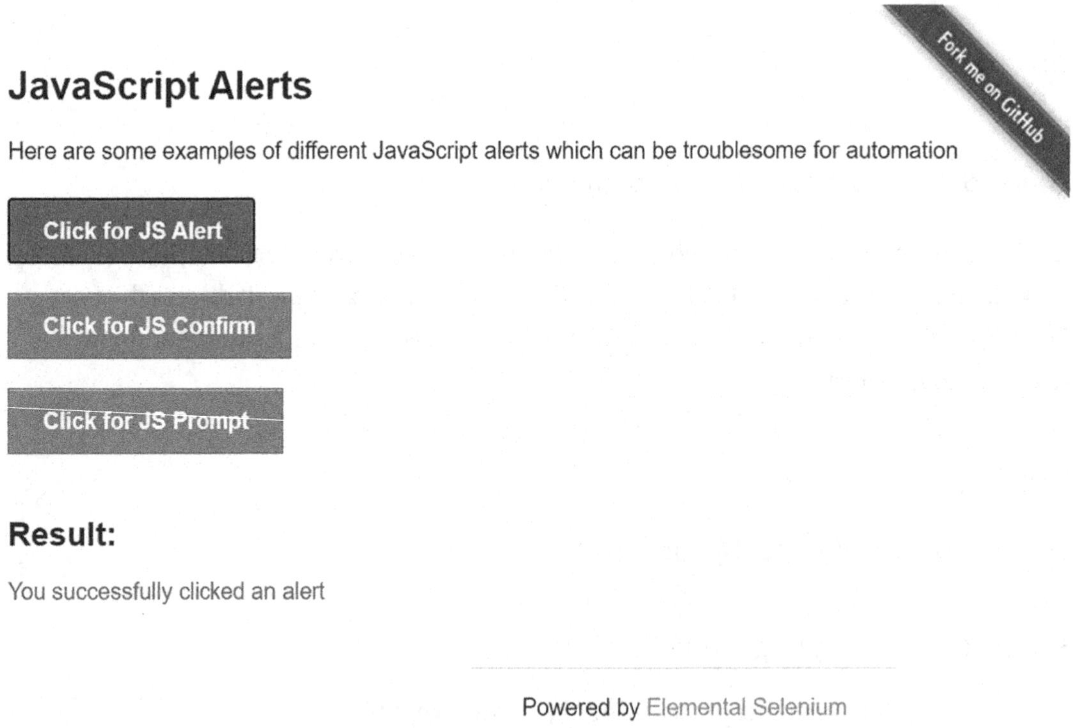

Figure 6-16.   *Success message after alert is handled*

Alerts: Dismissing an Alert

The next action on an alert box is to dismiss it by clicking Cancel, Dismiss, or any similar UI option provided by the web site, as shown in Figure 6-17.

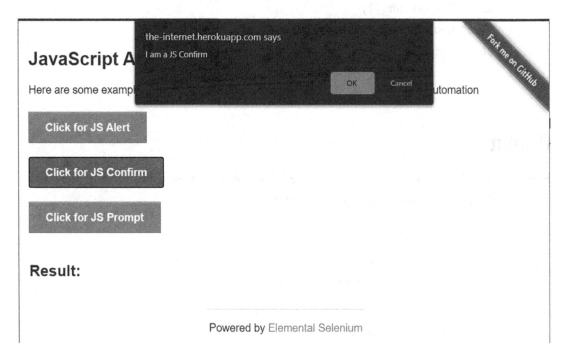

Figure 6-17. *Confirmation box with OK and Cancel as choice*

A dismiss option is available in the confirmation box. It can be automated, as shown in Listing 6-11.

Syntax

```
browser.switchTo().alert().dismiss();
```

Listing 6-11. Dismissing an Alert

```
it('Handling alerts:Dismiss an alert', async function () {
    browser.waitForAngularEnabled(false);
    await browser.driver.get('https://the-internet.herokuapp.com/
    javascript_alerts');
```

```
await browser.element(by.css('button[onclick="jsConfirm()"]')).click();
await browser.switchTo().alert().dismiss();
await browser.takeScreenshot().then(function (element) {
    let stream = fs.createWriteStream('./screenshots/
    alertdismiss.png');
    stream.write(new Buffer.from(element, 'base64'));
    stream.end();
})
})
```

Output

Figure 6-18 is the success message generated in the web page's UI to show the alert was successfully dismissed using the Cancel button.

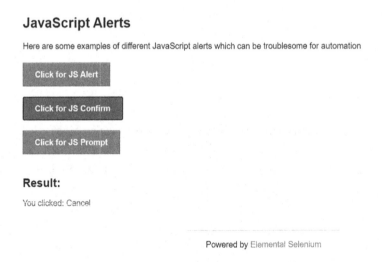

Figure 6-18. *Success message pops up after alert is dismissed*

Alerts: Sending Message to an Alert

A *prompt box* is another type of pop-up box used in JavaScript, as shown in Figure 6-19. It takes user input.

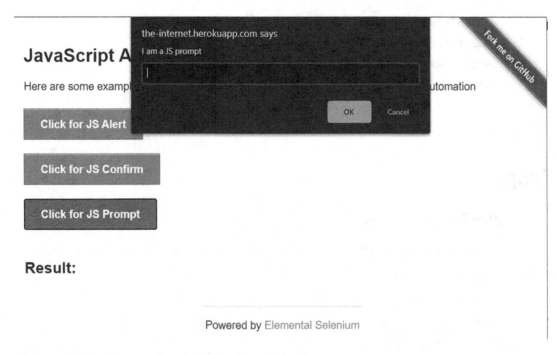

Figure 6-19. *Prompt box with input field*

After entering the input, the user must click OK to proceed, as shown in Listing 6-12. User will get the entered text on the webpage as shown in Figure 6-20. User can also click on the Cancel button, which will return a 'null' value on the webpage.

Syntax

```
browser.switchTo().alert().sendKeys("<input text>");
```

Listing 6-12. Sending Text from an Alert

```
it('Handling alerts:Dismiss an alert', async function () {
    browser.waitForAngularEnabled(false);
    await browser.driver.get('https://the-internet.herokuapp.com/
    javascript_alerts');
    await browser.element(by.css('button[onclick="jsPrompt()"]')).click();
    await browser.switchTo().alert().sendKeys("Text sent");
    await browser.switchTo().alert().accept()
    await browser.takeScreenshot().then(function (element) {
```

```
        let stream = fs.createWriteStream('./screenshots/
        alertsendtext.png');
        stream.write(new Buffer.from(element, 'base64'));
        stream.end();
    })
})
```

Output

JavaScript Alerts

Here are some examples of different JavaScript alerts which can be troublesome for automation

Click for JS Alert

Click for JS Confirm

Click for JS Prompt

Result:

You entered: Text sent

Powered by Elemental Selenium

Figure 6-20. *Input captured from alert is displayed*

Getting an HTML Element's ID

getId() method returns an HTML element's ID on a web page. Figure 6-21 shows the Go button has an ID associated with it.

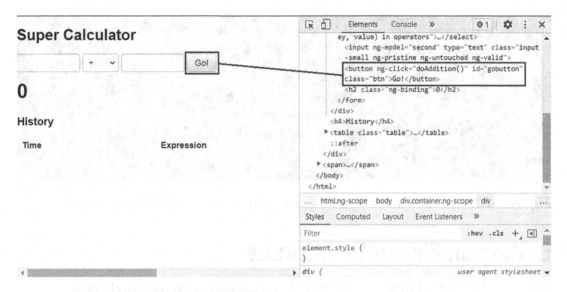

Figure 6-21. *The Go button HTML code*

Listing 6-13 locates the Go button through its class and fetches its ID.

Syntax

```
element(by.<locator>('<value>')).getId())
```

Listing 6-13. Fetching the ID of an Element

```
it('Get ID of an element', async function () {
    await browser.get('http://juliemr.github.io/protractor-demo/');
    console.log("ID is " + await element(by.className('btn')).getId())
    await browser.close()
})
```

Output

There was an issue with this method in the Protractor version used in this book. As you can see in Figure 6-22, the returned ID is not per expectations. However, you can achieve the same objective with the getAttribute API, which you see in the next example.

```
PS F:\AUTOMATION\Protractor> protractor conf.js
[12:20:57] I/launcher - Running 1 instances of WebDriver
[12:20:57] I/hosted - Using the selenium server at http://localhost:4444/wd/hub
Started
ID is 0.0006249931792325913-1


1 spec, 0 failures
Finished in 21.134 seconds
```

Figure 6-22. Console output of getId() method in current Protractor version

Getting an Element's Attribute

Using getAttribute() method, you can get the attributes of any HTML element, including the ID. Figure 6-23 shows some common attributes usually found in the DOM.

Attribute	Description
alt	Specifies an alternative text for an image
disabled	Specifies that an input element should be disabled
href	Specifies the URL (web address) for a link
id	Specifies a unique id for an element
src	Specifies the URL (web address) for an image
style	Specifies an inline CSS style for an element
title	Specifies extra information about an element (displayed as a tool tip)
value	Specifies the value (text content) for an input element.

Figure 6-23. Common attributes usually found in the DOM

Syntax

```
element(by.<locator>('<value>')).getAttribute('<value>')
```

Listing 6-14. Gets the Attribute of the HTML Element

```
it('Get attribute(ID) of an element', async function () {
    await browser.get('http://juliemr.github.io/protractor-demo/');
    console.log("ID is " + await element(by.className('btn')).
    getAttribute('id'))
    await browser.close()
})
```

Output

Figure 6-24 shows the ID attribute of the HTML element fetched and printed in the console terminal.

```
PS F:\AUTOMATION\Protractor> protractor conf.js
[12:35:24] I/launcher - Running 1 instances of WebDriver
[12:35:24] I/hosted - Using the selenium server at http://localhost:4444/wd/hub
Started
ID is gobutton

1 spec, 0 failures
Finished in 1.949 seconds
```

Figure 6-24. *ID of the HTML element*

This method can also fetch all the links on the web page in combination with the .each() method, as shown in Listing 6-15.

Listing 6-15. Getting All the Links on the Web Page

```
it('Get all links on the web page', async function () {
    await browser.get('https://www.protractortest.org/')
    await element.all(by.tagName('a')).each(async function (item) {
        console.log(await item.getAttribute('href'))
    })
})
```

As you can see in Figure 6-25, all the links available on the web page were fetched and shown on the console terminal.

```
PS F:\AUTOMATION\Protractor> protractor conf.js
[13:16:07] I/launcher - Running 1 instances of WebDriver
[13:16:07] I/hosted - Using the selenium server at http://localhost:4444/wd/hub
Started
https://www.protractortest.org/#/
javascript:void(0)
https://www.protractortest.org/#/tutorial
javascript:void(0)
https://www.protractortest.org/#/protractor-setup
https://www.protractortest.org/#/server-setup
https://www.protractortest.org/#/browser-setup
https://www.protractortest.org/#/frameworks
javascript:void(0)
https://www.protractortest.org/#/getting-started
https://www.protractortest.org/#/tutorial
https://www.protractortest.org/#/api-overview
https://www.protractortest.org/#/system-setup
https://www.protractortest.org/#/locators
https://www.protractortest.org/#/page-objects
https://www.protractortest.org/#/debugging
javascript:void(0)
https://github.com/angular/protractor/blob/master/lib/config.ts
https://www.protractortest.org/#/api
https://www.protractortest.org/#/style-guide
https://www.protractortest.org/#/webdriver-vs-protractor
https://www.protractortest.org/#/browser-support
https://www.protractortest.org/#/plugins
https://www.protractortest.org/#/timeouts
https://www.protractortest.org/#/control-flow
https://www.protractortest.org/#/typescript
https://www.protractortest.org/#/async-await
https://www.protractortest.org/#/infrastructure
https://www.protractortest.org/#/jasmine-upgrade
https://www.protractortest.org/#/mobile-setup
https://www.protractortest.org/#/faq
https://github.com/angular/protractor
https://twitter.com/ProtractorTest
http://localhost:4444/wd/hub
https://www.protractortest.org/#/tutorial


1 spec, 0 failures
```

Figure 6-25. *List of links fetched from the web page*

Getting the Tag Name

The getTagName() method fetches the tag name of the element if you reuse the code in Listing 6-14 and get the tag name of the element with the btn class (see Listing 6-16).

Syntax

```
element(by.<locator>('<value')).getTagName('<value>'))
```

Listing 6-16. Fetching the Tag Name of the Element

```
it('Get Tag Name of an element', async function () {
    await browser.get('http://juliemr.github.io/protractor-demo/');
    console.log("Tagname is " + await element(by.className('btn')).
    getTagName('id'))
    await browser.close()
})
```

Output

The element's tag name is fetched in the console terminal, as shown in Figure 6-26.

```
PS F:\AUTOMATION\Protractor> protractor conf.js
[13:29:10] I/launcher - Running 1 instances of WebDriver
[13:29:10] I/hosted - Using the selenium server at http://localhost:4444/wd/hub
Started
Tagname is button
.


1 spec, 0 failures
Finished in 6.001 seconds
```

Figure 6-26. *Tag name printed in the console terminal*

Getting the CSS Property

getCssValue() method fetches the CSS properties of the attribute. Attributes are written in the HTML and are associated with a specific element. However, when the browser parses the HTML code, a corresponding DOM node is created. This node is an object, and therefore it has properties associated with it. They can be seen in the Chrome DevTools console, as shown in Figure 6-27.

Figure 6-27. *CSS properties of Navbar-header element*

Syntax

```
element(by.<locator>('<value>')).getCssValue('<value>')
```

Listing 6-17. Fetching the Tag Name of the Element

```
it('Get Tag Name of an element', async function () {
    await browser.get('https://www.protractortest.org/#/');
    console.log("Font Family is " + await element(by.className(
    'navbar-header')).getCssValue('font-family'))
    await browser.close()
})
```

Output

The element's font family is fetched in the console terminal, as shown in Figure 6-28.

```
PS F:\AUTOMATION\Protractor> protractor conf.js
[13:49:53] I/launcher - Running 1 instances of WebDriver
[13:49:53] I/hosted - Using the selenium server at http://localhost:4444/wd/hub
Started
Font Family is "Helvetica Neue", Helvetica, Arial, sans-serif
.

1 spec, 0 failures
Finished in 5.046 seconds
```

Figure 6-28. *Font family printed in the console terminal*

The HTML `<img>` element can have the `width` or `height` attribute, and it can also have the CSS width/height properties.

```
<img src="abc.jpg" width="100" height="100"
style="width: 100px; height: 100px"></img>
```

Both parameters (height and width) work the same in attributes and properties when the image is rendered on the web page. However, some developers prefer to use as many parameters as they can in properties to keep their HTML code clean.

Summary

In this chapter, you looked at almost all the major APIs and functions provided by Protractor to mimic user interaction with web browsers. In the next chapter, you learn about assertions and the various ways to verify expected results from the actual results during the execution.

CHAPTER 7

Jasmine and Selenium Assertions

This chapter discusses assertions. In automation, the validations in test scripts are known as *assertions*. Node.js has a built-in assertion library that is called as follows: `const assert = require(assert)`. No installation is required. However, Protractor uses Jasmine's assertions to perform validations. You will look at the following examples in this chapter.

- Expected result is equal to the actual result

- Expected result is the actual result

- Expected result is positive

- Expected result is negative

- Negative matchers with not

- Validate if expected result is null, NaN, and so forth

- Custom matchers

Verifying If Strings Match by Value

Listing 7-1 shows a simple example where the user navigates to the Super Calculator web page, locates the heading (h3) element on the web page (see Figure 7-1), and verifies/asserts if it is equal to the value provided.

© Shashank Shukla 2021
S. Shukla, *The Protractor Handbook*, https://doi.org/10.1007/978-1-4842-7289-3_7

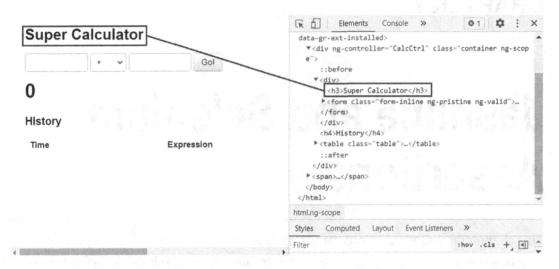

Figure 7-1. Super Calculator heading element

Listing 7-1. Jasmine assertion toEqual

```
it('Validate the Header of the Web page', function () {
    browser.get('http://juliemr.github.io/protractor-demo/');
    let headingText = element(by.tagName('h3')).getText()
    expect(headingText).toEqual("Super Calculator");
})
```

Output

Figure 7-2 shows both my failed attempt—where I made a typo (Super Calculator)—and a following successful attempt (see Listing 7-1).

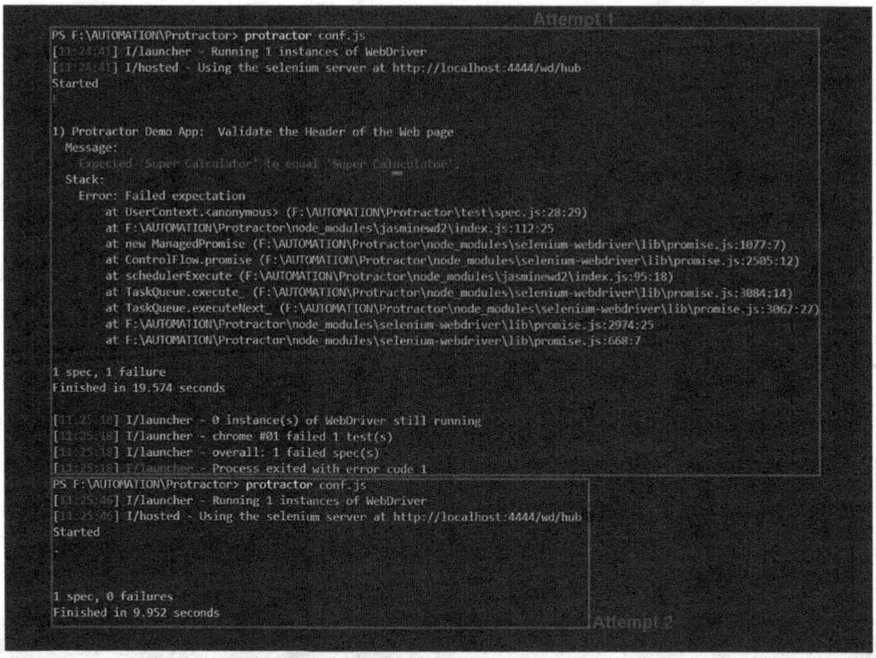

Figure 7-2. *Assertion pass and fail comparison*

EXERCISE

Validate the button text on the Super Calculator web page.

Verifying If Expected Result and Actual Results Are Same

In Node.js, two objects can look the same but are not the same. For instance, if you save the {name: Ryu} object literal in both the a and b variables and then check if a is equal to b using expect(a).toEqual(b);, it passes the test script. However, if you use expect(a).toBe(b);, it fails (see Listing 7-2).

Listing 7-2. Jasmine Assertion toBe

```
it('Using toBe assertion', function () {
    var a = { name: 'Ryu' };
    var b = { name: 'Ryu' };
    expect(a).toBe(b);
})
```

Output

Figure 7-3 shows the expected failed message to let the user know that variable a is not variable b even though they have equal values, implying that toEqual() compares by content and toBe() compares by object reference. Typically, they can be used interchangeably when dealing with primitive types (string, number, boolean, etc.).

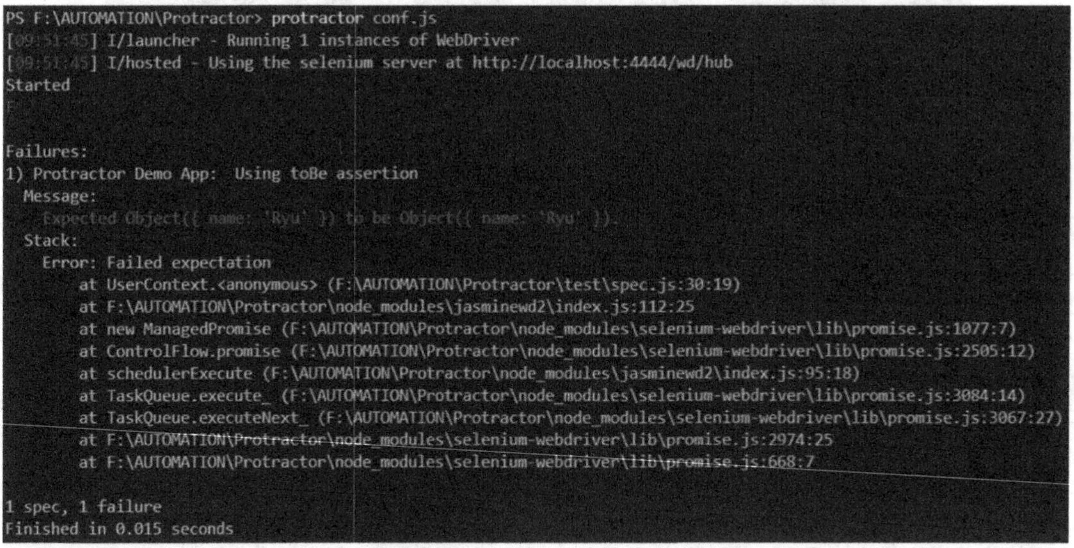

Figure 7-3. *Assertion fail message*

Verifying If the Values Are Truthy or Falsy

The word *truthy* means that it tends to be true if not completely true. In Listing 7-3, the expected value on the left-hand side is a random string that passes the assertion as truthy. The following are some others examples of truthy values: 100, abc, True, and { }.

Listing 7-3. Asserting Actual to Be Truthy

```
it('Using Truthy assertion', function () {
    expect('a random string').toBeTruthy();
})
```

Listing 7-4 is successfully executed as `false` (boolean). It is a falsy value. It also executes without any error if you provide values like null, "", 0, undefined, and NaN, because they are falsy values too.

Listing 7-4. Asserting Actual To Be Falsy

```
it('Using False assertion', function () {
    expect('').toBeFalsy();
})
```

Verifying If a String Is Present with toContain

The `toContain` assertion validates if an element contains a specific value/string that the user is expecting. In Listing 7-5, the example locates the heading of the Super Calculator web page and validates if it contains the "Super" string.

Listing 7-5. Jasmine Assertion toContain

```
it('Using toContain assertion', function () {
    browser.get('http://juliemr.github.io/protractor-demo/');
    let headingText = element(by.tagName('h3')).getText()
    expect(headingText).toContain("Super");
})
```

Output

Figure 7-4 shows that the test case successfully executed.

```
PS F:\AUTOMATION\Protractor> protractor conf.js
[11:11:57] I/launcher - Running 1 instances of WebDriver
[11:11:57] I/hosted - Using the selenium server at http://localhost:4444/wd/hub
Started
.


1 spec, 0 failures
Finished in 13.299 seconds
```

Figure 7-4. *Console terminal showing the test case executed successfully*

The API can also validate if an element is a member of an array. Consider the following examples, which successfully execute.

```
expect([1, 2, 3, 4]).toContain(4);
expect(["Penguin", "Turtle", "Panda", "Duck"]).toContain("Duck");
```

Negating Matchers

All the assertions you have looked at so far can be negated by using the not keyword. It's useful to reverse Jasmine's matchers to make sure that they aren't true. To do that, simply use the .toContain prefix in Listing 7-5 with .not, as shown in Listing 7-6.

Listing 7-6. Jasmine Assertion Using not

```
it('Using toContain assertion', function () {
    browser.get('http://juliemr.github.io/protractor-demo/');
    let headingText = element(by.tagName('h3')).getText()
    expect(headingText).not.toContain("Super");
})
```

Output

Figure 7-5 fails as expected because the "Super" string is part of the "Super Calculator" heading element.

```
PS F:\AUTOMATION\Protractor> protractor conf.js
[11:24:35] I/launcher - Running 1 instances of WebDriver
[11:24:35] I/hosted - Using the selenium server at http://localhost:4444/wd/hub
Started
F

Failures:
1) Protractor Demo App: Using toContain assertion
  Message:
    Expected 'Super Calculator' not to contain 'Super'.
  Stack:
    Error: Failed expectation
        at UserContext.<anonymous> (F:\AUTOMATION\Protractor\test\spec.js:29:33)
        at F:\AUTOMATION\Protractor\node_modules\jasminewd2\index.js:112:25
        at new ManagedPromise (F:\AUTOMATION\Protractor\node_modules\selenium-webdriver\lib\promise.js:1077:7)
        at ControlFlow.promise (F:\AUTOMATION\Protractor\node_modules\selenium-webdriver\lib\promise.js:2505:12)
        at schedulerExecute (F:\AUTOMATION\Protractor\node_modules\jasminewd2\index.js:95:18)
        at TaskQueue.execute_ (F:\AUTOMATION\Protractor\node_modules\selenium-webdriver\lib\promise.js:3084:14)
        at TaskQueue.executeNext_ (F:\AUTOMATION\Protractor\node_modules\selenium-webdriver\lib\promise.js:3067:27)
        at F:\AUTOMATION\Protractor\node_modules\selenium-webdriver\lib\promise.js:2974:25
        at F:\AUTOMATION\Protractor\node_modules\selenium-webdriver\lib\promise.js:668:7

1 spec, 1 failure
Finished in 11 seconds
```

Figure 7-5. *Failed assertion message*

Some Other Interesting Matchers

Jasmine provides a long list of matchers that are useful for automation during result verification. For more information, see https://jasmine.github.io/api/3.7/matchers.

The following are some of the commonly used matchers.

```
expect(null).Bernoulli();               // success
expect(8).toBeGreaterThan(5);           // success
expect(5).toBeLessThan(12);             // success
expect([1,2]).toHaveSize(2) ;           // success
```

Is the Element Present?: isPresent()

isPresent() (or isElementPresent()) is a Selenium method used by Protractor to check the presence of a web element on a web page.

Figure 7-6 shows that the web page's source code doesn't have an h1 element.

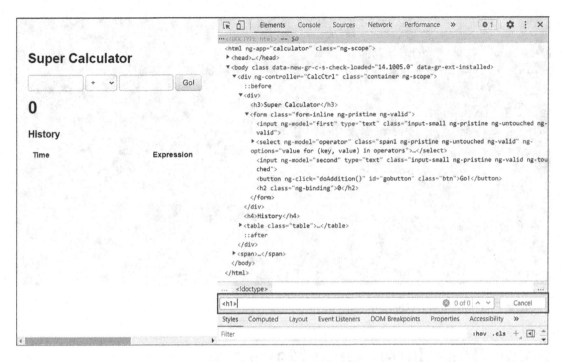

Figure 7-6. *Returned result of h1 element on web page*

When the presence of an h1 element is checked, the `isPresent` method should return `false` (see Listing 7-7).

Listing 7-7. Verifying <h1> Tag's Presence on the Page

```
it('Using isPresent to verify elements presence on webpage', async
function () {
    await browser.get('http://juliemr.github.io/protractor-demo/');
    let h1 = await element(by.tagName('h1')).isPresent()
    console.log("Presence of <H1> tag on webpage:- " + h1)
    expect(h1).toBe(false);
})
```

Output

Listing 7-7 printed a "Presence of <H1> tag on webpage: false" console output and asserted the value of the h1 variable to the expected result (i.e., false).

isPresent is technically not an assertion itself (it's an element API) but a crucial step before an assertion to find the presence of an element on a web page and passing or failing the test script accordingly, as shown in Figure 7-7.

```
PS F:\AUTOMATION\Protractor> protractor conf.js
[12:03:59] I/launcher - Running 1 instances of WebDriver
[12:03:59] I/hosted - Using the selenium server at http://localhost:4444/wd/hub
Started
Presence of <H1> tag on webpage:- false


1 spec, 0 failures
Finished in 1.822 seconds
```

Figure 7-7. *Console output of the state of the element*

In real-life scenarios, a better example of the isPresent() API is an animation-heavy web page that interacts with an element and needs to wait for the element to load in the DOM.

EXERCISE

Go to https://the-internet.herokuapp.com/dynamic_loading/2 and follow these steps, as also shown in Figure 7-8.

Step 1. Click the Start button.

Step 2. Print the status of the presence of the Hello World text.

Step 3. Wait 10 seconds and print the status of the presence of Hello World text.

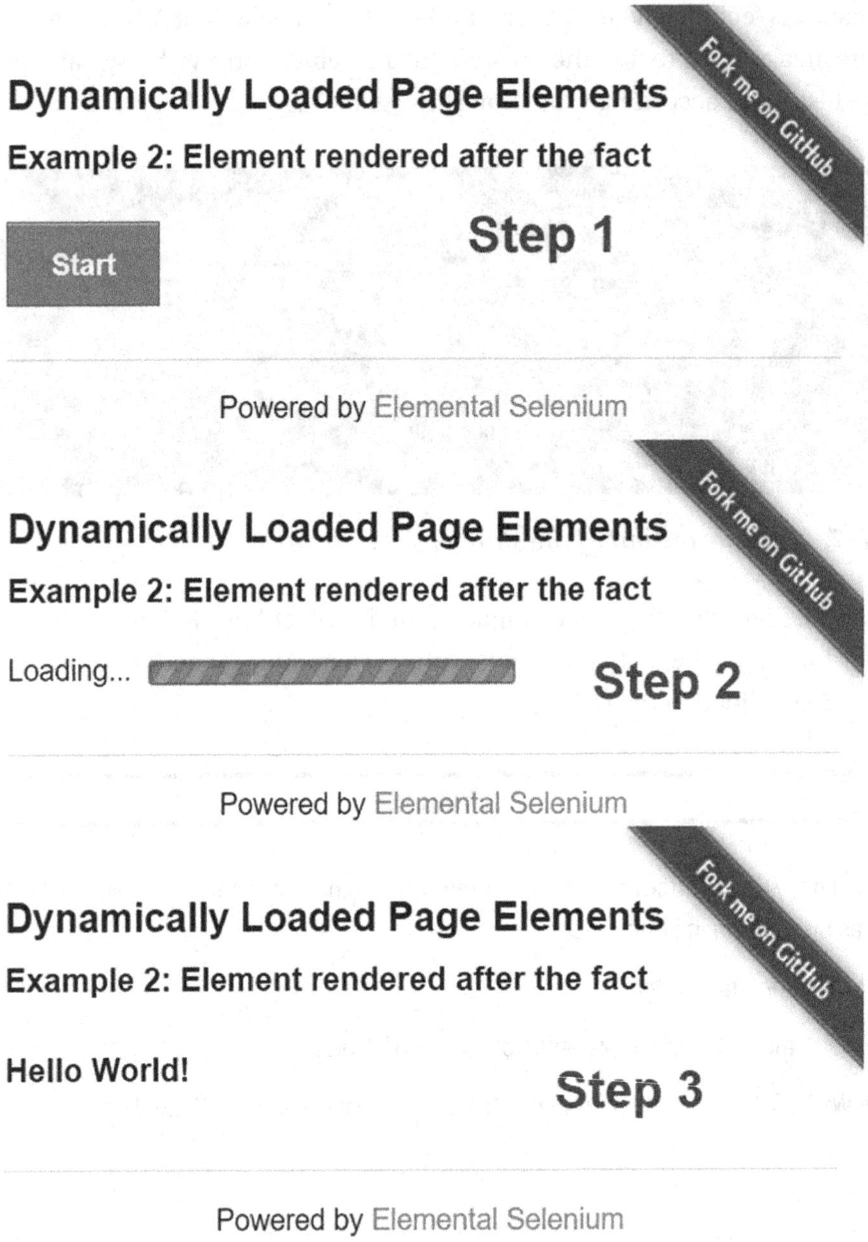

Figure 7-8. *Comparing the states of an element that appears in DOM after few seconds*

The difference between an element API like `isPresent` and an assertion like `Expect` is that the former never fails the test case when returning `false`; however, the latter would fail the test case if the expected doesn't match the actual result, even if the expected result is `true`.

Is the Element Selected?: isSelected()

The `isSelected()` method is usually verifies whether the checkboxes are checked (selected), as shown in Figure 7-9. This is not an assertion; hence, it only returns `true` or `false` values. How you want to handle it is up to you.

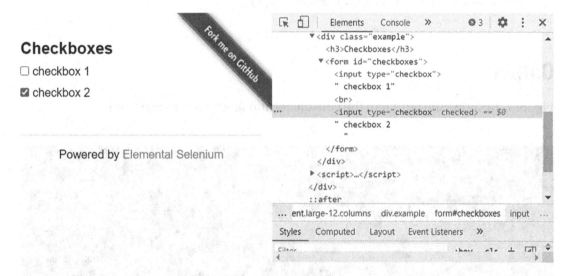

Figure 7-9. *Checkboxes present on the web page*

Two checkboxes are dealt with in Listing 7-8, where the first checkbox is unchecked and the second is checked. Web developers use the `selected` or checked property `<input type="checkbox" checked="">`. You can see the difference in the HTML code between an unchecked (checkbox 1) and a checked (checkbox 2) box. You locate and apply the `isSelected()` method on both checkbox elements and get an output of `true` and `false`, respectively, as expected.

Syntax

`isSelected()`

Listing 7-8. Using Element API isSelected()

```
it('Using isSelected to verify checkbox is checked on webpage',
async function () {
    await browser.waitForAngularEnabled(false);
    await browser.get('https://the-internet.herokuapp.com/checkboxes');
    let ChkBox1 = await element.all(by.css('input[type="checkbox"]')).get(0)
    console.log('Verifying if the First Checkbox is selected = ')
    console.log(await ChkBox1.isSelected())
    let ChkBox2 = await element.all(by.css('input[type="checkbox"]')).get(1)
    console.log('Verifying if the Second Checkbox is selected = ')
    console.log(await ChkBox2.isSelected())
})
```

Output

Figure 7-10 shows the output in the console terminal, which is as expected.

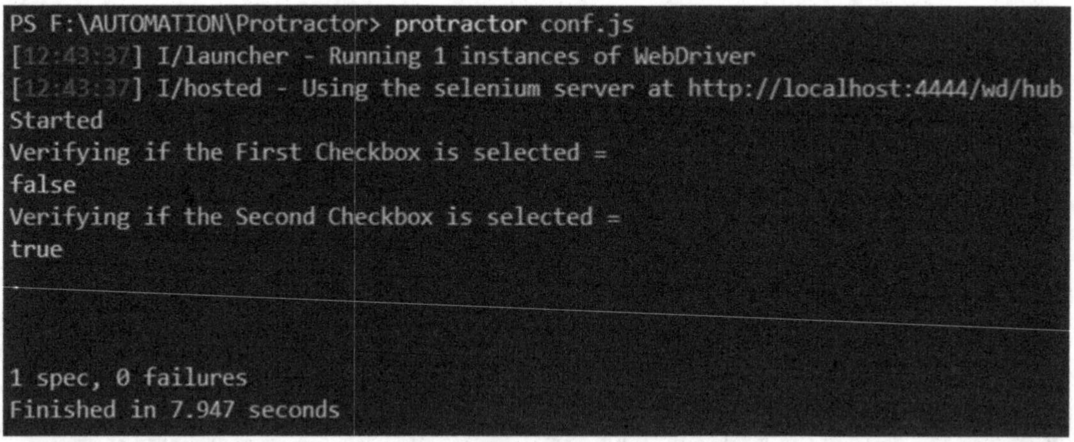

Figure 7-10. *The output in the console*

Is the Element Enabled?: isEnabled()

Web developers can enable or disabled certain element tags by modifying the `disabled` element property in `<input type="text" disabled="disabled" />`. This is primarily used for elements like radio buttons and input fields. You can check if an element is enabled or disabled by using the `isEnabled()` method. Figure 7-11 shows a disabled, grayed-out textbox.

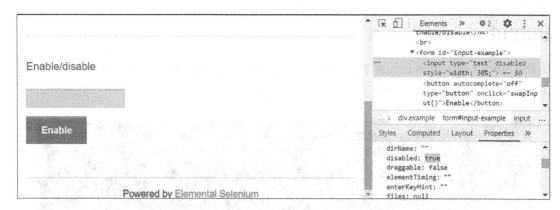

Figure 7-11. *Disabled text box present on the web page*

Listing 7-9 navigates to the URL and identifies the disabled input text field. Following that, you use the `isEnabled()` method to print the status of the field before clicking the Enable button. In the next step, you click the Enable button in the UI and then again, after 5 seconds, apply the `isEnabled()` method to print the result.

Syntax

```
isEnabled()
```

Listing 7-9. Using Element API isEnabled()

```
it('Using isEnabled to verify element is enabled on webpage', async
function () {
    await browser.waitForAngularEnabled(false);
    await browser.get('https://the-internet.herokuapp.com/
    dynamic_controls');
    let elem = await element(by.css('input[type="text"]'))
```

```
console.log('Verifying element is Enabled before clicking button=')
console.log(await elem.isEnabled())
await element(by.css("button[onclick='swapInput()']")).click()
await browser.sleep(5000)
console.log('Verifying element is Enabled after clicking button= ')
console.log(await elem.isEnabled())
})
```

Output

In the output shown in Figure 7-12, the first isEnabled() method returns false. It returns true the second time.

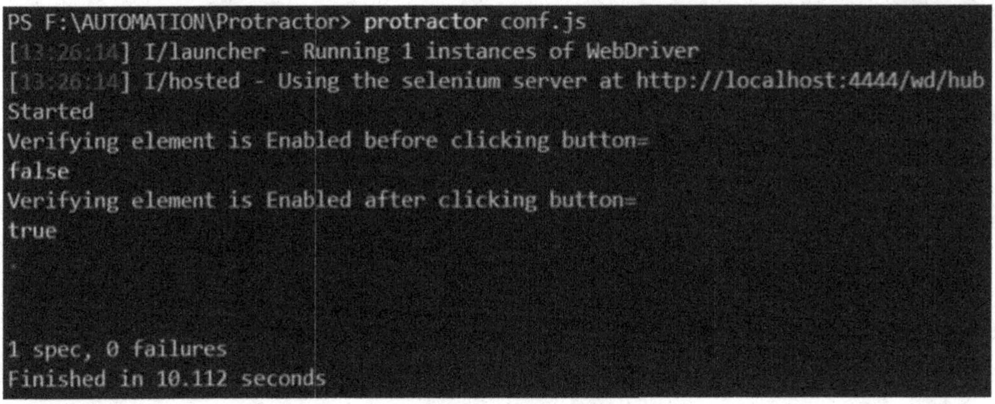

Figure 7-12. *Console output comparing the state of element*

If you apply a debug checkpoint on the last line of code and inspect the input element, you see that the disabled property is false, as shown in Figure 7-13.

Figure 7-13. *Difference in <input> tag HTML code after Enable button is clicked*

Notes

isEnabled() checks for the disabled attribute in a property. If the button is disabled by any other means, isEnabled() might not work.

Is the Element Visible?: isDisplayed()

There are times when elements are present on a web page but are hidden. The isDisplayed() method identifies if the element is hidden or visible and provides a response in the form of the true or false boolean. Observe the Start button in Figure 7-14.

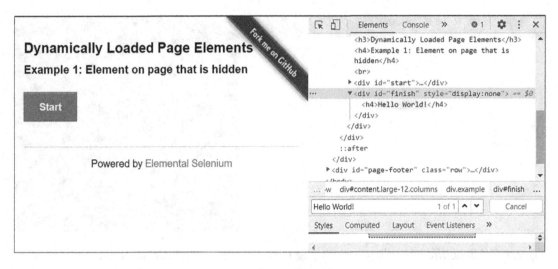

Figure 7-14. *Start button present on the web page*

Listing 7-10 shows isDisplayed() in action, where the user navigates to a URL and clicks the Start button. Since the Start button is dynamic and takes some time to make the hidden element visible, you verify it immediately after clicking the Start button and get a false output as expected. After 7 seconds, apply isDisplayed() again, and you get the true expected response because the element has become visible by then.

Syntax

isDisplayed()

Listing 7-10. Using Element API isDisplayed()

```
it('Using isDisplayed to verify element is enabled on webpage',
async function () {
    await browser.waitForAngularEnabled(false);
    await browser.get('https://the-internet.herokuapp.com/
    dynamic_loading/1');
    await element(by.tagName('button')).click()
    let elem = await element(by.id('finish'))
    console.log('Visibility of element: Right after Start button is
    clicked: ')
    console.log(await elem.isDisplayed())
```

```
    await browser.sleep(7000)
    console.log('Visibility of element: After 7 second pause: ')
    console.log(await elem.isDisplayed())
})
```

Output

As you can see in Figure 7-15, after 7 seconds of delay, when the element appears on the web page, the isDisplayed method returns true.

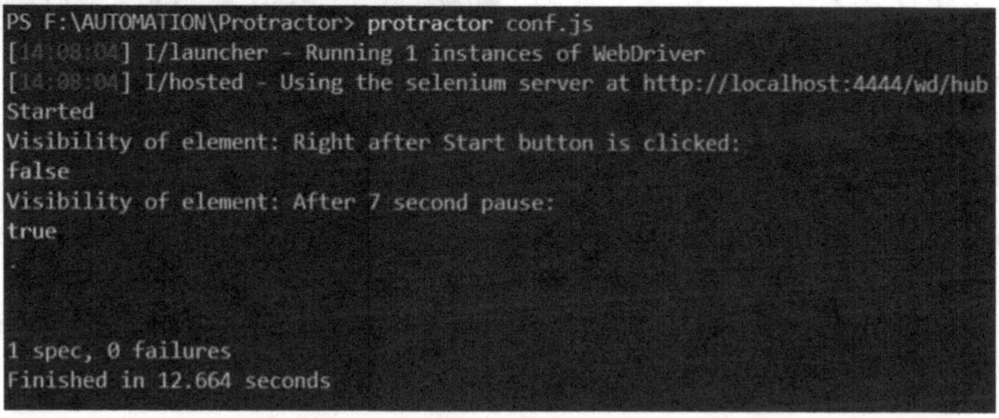

Figure 7-15. *Shows the output in the console*

Look out for elements with visibility: hidden, or opacity: 0, or the display: none property in Styles, which are common tactics used by web developers to hide elements in web pages. Figure 7-16 shows the element's state if the execution is paused by the debugger; the display: none style property seen in Figure 7-14 is now gone.

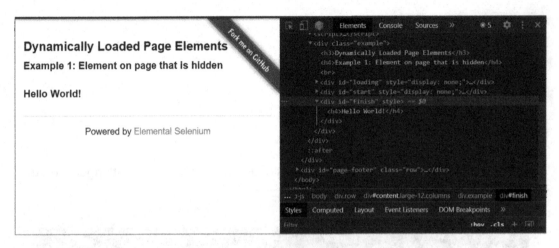

Figure 7-16. *State of <div> with id finish after Start button is clicked*

Summary

In this chapter, you learned about Jasmine assertions and some Protractor API methods. You can use these APIs between successfully locating an element and interacting with it.

In the next chapter, you learn about waits and timeouts and how to avoid using the hard waits that you have used so far.

CHAPTER 8

Waits and Timeouts

This chapter discusses waits. Unreliability in tests occurs due to rare conditions between the browser and the automation tool's instructions. There are times when the browser lags, and the automation tool's instructions are executed even when the element is not yet available in the DOM. Sometimes the element loads after a few seconds, depending on the network bandwidth server response time or how animation-intensive the web page is.

This chapter examines three ways to handle waits in Protractor or Selenium.

- Hard waits

- Explicit waits

- Implicit waits

Hard and Explicit Waits at a Glance

Using hard-coded waits (static waits) before every statement (as you have done using the `browser.sleep(milliseconds)` command) is bad practice because it slows down the whole suite's execution, which is particularly noticeable if your test suite has thousands of tests to run.

A smarter approach uses dynamic waits, like implicit and explicit waits, because they are reliable and faster. Dynamic waits always wait until the object/state is resolved through promises and relies on actual object availability. It is generally faster if implemented correctly.

© Shashank Shukla 2021
S. Shukla, *The Protractor Handbook*, https://doi.org/10.1007/978-1-4842-7289-3_8

Hard Waits

Listing 8-1 shows that after clicking the Submit button, you wait for 10 seconds before the text "Hello World" appears. However, the text appears a lot sooner than 10 seconds but the script waits for 10 seconds anyway—wasting time that could have been put into executing. Even then, a hard wait may not work in scenarios where the application is slow or there is an issue with the user's Internet speed.

The only fair use of a hard wait allows you to observe your test case flow while you are developing it; however, the debug option you saw earlier is still a better solution. In this chapter, you remove the wait statements in examples to observe the kinds of errors that you encounter.

Syntax

```
browser.sleep(milliseconds)
```

Listing 8-1. Hard Sleep of 10 Seconds Applied in the Test Script

```
it('Fixed execution pause duration', async function () {
    await browser.waitForAngularEnabled(false);
    await browser.get('https://the-internet.herokuapp.com/
    dynamic_loading/1')
    await element(by.tagName('button')).click()
    await browser.sleep(10000)
    console.log("Hidden Text is:")
    console.log(await element.all(by.tagName('h4')).get(1).getText())
})
```

Output

Since this is a hard wait, Protractor pauses the execution and always waits for 10 seconds before resuming the execution, which causes the script to run slowly. It takes a long time to finish the script (see Figure 8-1).

```
PS F:\AUTOMATION\Protractor> protractor conf.js
[11:46:12] I/launcher - Running 1 instances of WebDriver
[11:46:12] I/hosted - Using the selenium server at http://localhost:4444/wd/hub
Started
Hidden Text is:
Hello World!



1 spec, 0 failures
Finished in 14.531 seconds
```

Figure 8-1. *Hello World printed along with total time the test script took to*
execute

Explicit Wait: Wait for an Element to Be Displayed

Let's use the last example again. Instead of waiting for 10 seconds, you want to fetch
the text "Hello World" as soon as it is visible in the UI. In Protractor, you use *expected*
conditions (derived from Selenium) to achieve this objective. Expected conditions
provide functionalities to wait for certain conditions. Listing 8-2 demonstrates an
explicit wait, which waits for the element to become visible. The maximum wait timeout
is 10,000 milliseconds, or 10 seconds. Once the Start button is pressed, the element is
visible within a few seconds (see Figure 8-2). It is fetched via getText and displayed in
the terminal through console.log.

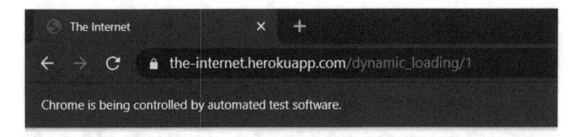

Dynamically Loaded Page Elements

Example 1: Element on page that is hidden

Start

Figure 8-2. Start button displays Hello World! after a slight pause once clicked

Syntax

```
browser.wait(await EC.visibilityOf(element (by.<locator>('<value>'))),
<timeout>);
```

Listing 8-2. Waiting for Hello World! to Be Visible After Clicking Start Button

```
it('Explicit/Conditional wait- Element to be displayed', async function () {
    await browser.waitForAngularEnabled(false);
    await browser.get('https://the-internet.herokuapp.com/
    dynamic_loading/1')
    await element(by.tagName('button')).click();
    let EC = await protractor.ExpectedConditions;
    browser.wait(await EC.visibilityOf(element.all(by.tagName('h4')).
    get(1)), 5000);
    console.log("Hidden Text is:")
    console.log(await element.all(by.tagName('h4')).get(1).getText())
})
```

Output

Figure 8-3 shows the difference in the runtime when comparing this execution to the one in Listing 8-1.

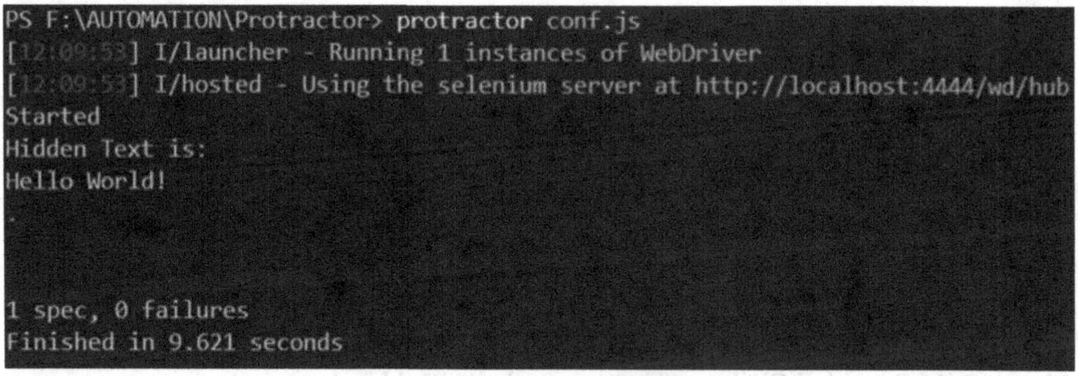

```
PS F:\AUTOMATION\Protractor> protractor conf.js
[12:09:53] I/launcher - Running 1 instances of WebDriver
[12:09:53] I/hosted - Using the selenium server at http://localhost:4444/wd/hub
Started
Hidden Text is:
Hello World!

1 spec, 0 failures
Finished in 9.621 seconds
```

Figure 8-3. *Total time of execution using dynamic wait*

The reverse of this method is the `invisibilityOf` method, where you need to wait for an element to become invisible before you can take the next step.

Wait for Element to Be Clickable

In Figure 8-4, the Click Me!!! button is enabled in the DOM after 3 seconds. This is achieved using the `disabled="true"` attribute. Listing 8-3 fetches the button by its ID and waits for it to be clickable. As soon as it is, the text displayed in the subsequent <p> tag can be fetched.

Figure 8-4.   *Disabled Click me!!! button at the initial load*

Syntax

```
browser.wait(await EC. elementToBeClickable (element
(by.<locator>('<value>'))), <timeout>);
```

Listing 8-3.   Waiting for Remove Button to Be Clickable

```
it('Explicit/Conditional wait- Element to be clickable', async function () {
    await browser.waitForAngularEnabled(false);
    await browser.get('https://output.jsbin.com/gecequg')
    let button = await element(by.id('MY_ID'))
    let EC = await protractor.ExpectedConditions;
    browser.wait(await EC.elementToBeClickable(button), 5000);
    await button.click()
    console.log("Text is:")
    console.log(await element(by.id('demo')).getText())
})
```

Output

`elementToBeClickable()` method always waits for the element to be clickable. It is a good practice to place it before clicking any button to ensure the button is not disabled. The code in Listing 8-3 should also be tried without the `elementToBeClickable()` method and differences in the results should be observed.

Wait for Text to Be Present in an Element Value

`textToBePresentInElementValue()` command ensures that Protractor waits until the text is present in the element's value attribute in the DOM before proceeding to the next step (see Figure 8-5).

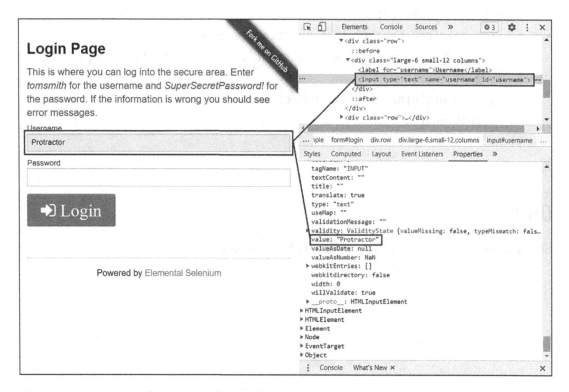

Figure 8-5. *Input element with text Protractor*

Listing 8-4 sends text to the input field and waits until the expected text is input before taking a screenshot. It uses `element(by.id(username))` (i.e., `$(#username)`) as shorthand.

Syntax

```
browser.wait(await EC.textToBePresentInElementValue(element
(by.<locator>('<value>'))), <timeout>);
```

Listing 8-4. Waiting for Input Field to Be Enabled After Clicking Enable Button

```
it('textToBePresentInElementValue', async function () {
    browser.waitForAngularEnabled(false);
    await browser.get('https://the-internet.herokuapp.com/login');
    await browser.$('#username').sendKeys("Protractor");
    var EC = await protractor.ExpectedConditions;
    await browser.wait(EC.textToBePresentInElementValue($('#username'),
    'Protractor'), 5000);
    browser.takeScreenshot().then(function (element) {
        let stream = fs.createWriteStream('./screenshots/texttobepresent.
        png');
        stream.write(new Buffer.from(element, 'base64'));
        stream.end();
    })
})
```

Output

Figure 8-6 shows the screenshot captured after the wait.

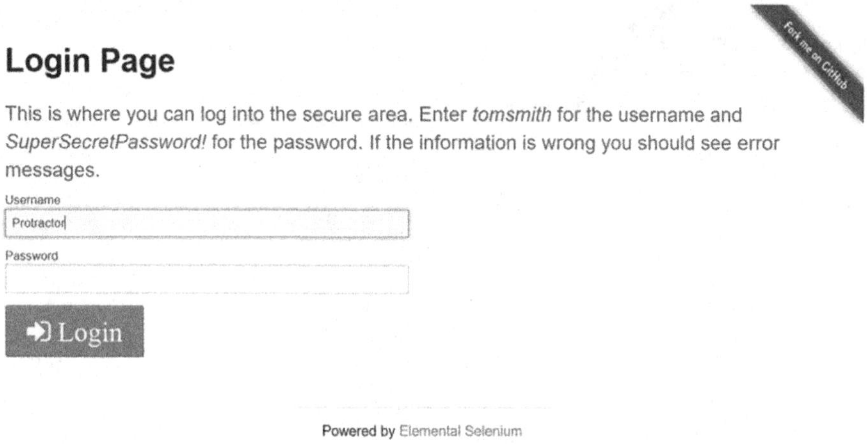

Login Page

This is where you can log into the secure area. Enter *tomsmith* for the username and *SuperSecretPassword!* for the password. If the information is wrong you should see error messages.

Username

Protractor

Password

➔) Login

Powered by Elemental Selenium

Figure 8-6. *Input box with Protractor text captured*

EXERCISE

Try to use `textToBePresentInElement` in the same example to wait for the `<h2>` element to have the Login Page text.

Wait for an Element to Exist

`presenceOf()` command waits until the element is rendered in the DOM before letting the control go further. Listing 8-5 waits for the h4 element to exist before printing it in the console. Once the Start button is clicked, the Hello World! element is rendered in the DOM inside the `<body>` tag from the `<script>` tag (see Figure 8-7).

Figure 8-7. *String Hello World! Is not present in the DOM yet*

Syntax

```
browser.wait(await EC.presenceOf(element (by.<locator>('<value>'))),
<timeout>);
```

Listing 8-5. Waiting for Input Field to Exist in Web Page DOM After Clicking
Finish Button

```
it('Explicit/Conditional wait- Element to exist in DOM', async function () {
    await browser.waitForAngularEnabled(false);
    await browser.get('https://the-internet.herokuapp.com/
    dynamic_loading/2')
    await element(by.tagName('button')).click();
    let EC = await protractor.ExpectedConditions;
    browser.wait(await EC.presenceOf(element.all(by.tagName('h4')).get(1)),
    5000);
    console.log("Text is:")
    console.log(await element.all(by.tagName('h4')).get(1).getText())
})
```

Output

Figure 8-8 shows the fetched element prints to the terminal as soon as it is rendered in the DOM and UI.

```
PS F:\AUTOMATION\Protractor> protractor conf.js
[13:46:32] I/launcher - Running 1 instances of WebDriver
[13:46:32] I/hosted - Using the selenium server at http://localhost:4444/wd/hub
Started
Text is:
Hello World!
.


1 spec, 0 failures
Finished in 9.887 seconds
```

Figure 8-8. *String Hello World! is not present in the DOM yet*

The reverse of this is the `stalenessOf` method, which is used when you must wait for an element to become stale and no longer present in the DOM.

Title Is/URL Is/Title Contains/URL Contains

There are a few simple methods that wait until a web page's URL and title has a specific string or substring, as shown in Listing 8-6.

Syntax

```
browser.wait(EC.titleIs('<value>'), <timeout>);
browser.wait(EC.titleContains('<value>'), <timeout>);
browser.wait(EC.urlIs('<value>'), <timeout>);
browser.wait(EC.urlContains('<value>'), <timeout>);
```

Listing 8-6. Waiting for Input Field to Exist in Web Page DOM After Clicking Finish Button

```
it('Title is & Title contains', async function () {
    await browser.waitForAngularEnabled(false);
    await browser.get('http://juliemr.github.io/protractor-demo/');
    let EC = await protractor.ExpectedConditions;
    await browser.wait(EC.titleContains('Super'), 5000);
    expect(browser.getTitle()).toBe('Super Calculator')
})
```

Output

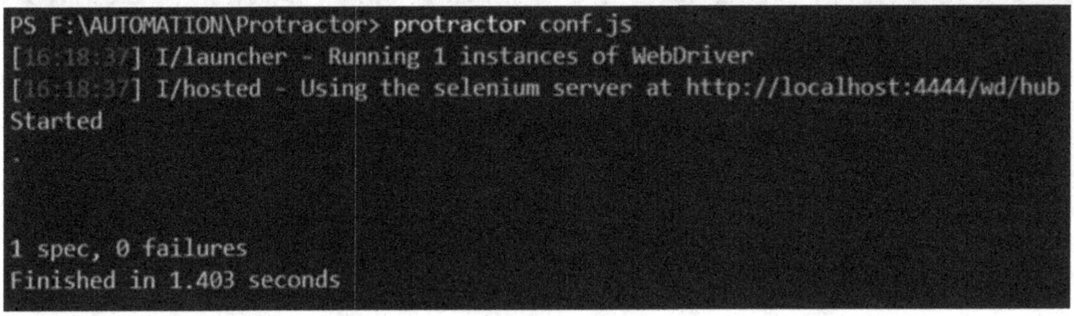

```
PS F:\AUTOMATION\Protractor> protractor conf.js
[16:18:37] I/launcher - Running 1 instances of WebDriver
[16:18:37] I/hosted - Using the selenium server at http://localhost:4444/wd/hub
Started


1 spec, 0 failures
Finished in 1.403 seconds
```

Figure 8-9. *Polling mechanism of waitUntil example in Listing 7-9*

Implicit Wait

An implicit wait in Protractor and Selenium tells the web driver to wait for a certain amount of time before throwing a "No Such Element Exception" error and to keep polling for the element's availability at certain time interval. An implicit wait is available for the entire elements and lifespan of the browser. It waits for an element for a maximum of 30 seconds, and then it must go ahead with the execution. The default Protractor timeout for an implicit wait is 500 milliseconds. It works for only the element and element.all (as soon as the first element displays) methods. Implicit wait should be placed under the describe block and not inside an it block (see Figure 8-10). Avoid mixing implicit and explicit waits as it can give an unexpected outcome and also considered a bad practice.

```
test > JS spec.js > ⊘ describe('Protractor Demo App: ') callback
  1    const { Buffer } = require('buffer');
  2    var fs = require('fs');
  3    const { browser, element } = require('protractor');
  4
  5  > async function addFun() { ···
 11    }
 12
 13  > async function subFun() { ···
 20    }
 21
 22    describe('Protractor Demo App: ', function () {
 23        browser.manage().timeouts().implicitlyWait(3000)
 24        it('Title is & Title contains', async function () {
 25            await browser.waitForAngularEnabled(false);
 26            await browser.get('http://juliemr.github.io/protractor-demo/');
 27            let EC = await protractor.ExpectedConditions;
 28            await browser.wait(EC.titleContains('Super'), 5000);
 29            expect(browser.getTitle()).toBe('Super Calculator');
 30        })
 31    });
 32
```

Figure 8-10. *Position of implicit wait in the test suite*

Timeouts: Protractor Waiting for Page to Load

pageLoadTimeout comes into play when waiting for Angular components to load onto the page. Before performing any action, Protractor waits until there are no pending asynchronous tasks in your Angular application. This means that all timeouts and HTTP requests are finished. If Angular components on the page take more than the specified time, the test script fails with the "E/protractor - Could not find Angular on page: retries looking for Angular exceeded" error. The default timeout parameter is 10,000 milliseconds, or 10 seconds. It can be implemented by adding getPageTimeout in the conf.js file, as shown in Figure 8-11.

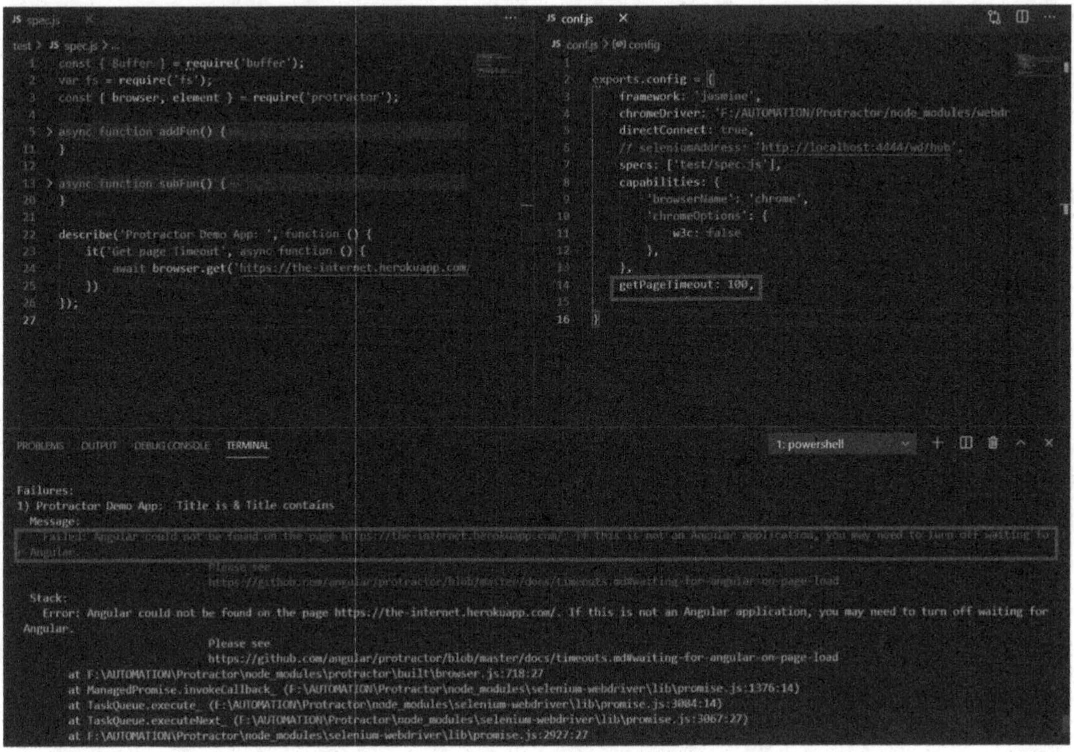

Figure 8-11. *Position of getPageTimeout in the test suite*

pageLoadTimeout can also be added by using the `browser.manage` (`driver.timeouts().pageloadTimeout(10000)` method in the spec file.

Timeouts: WebDriver allScriptsTimeout

allScriptsTimeout is a combined timeout in milliseconds for each script running on the browser. This should be longer than the maximum time your application needs to stabilize between tasks. `allScript` timeouts come into the picture on back-end Angular scripts triggered from your app. You do not see any difference in how your tests run if your app generally doesn't make behind-the-scenes script calls. A timeout waiting for an asynchronous Angular task is set as 11 seconds by default. It can be added as `allScriptsTimeout: timeout in milliseconds` in the Protractor `conf.js` file.

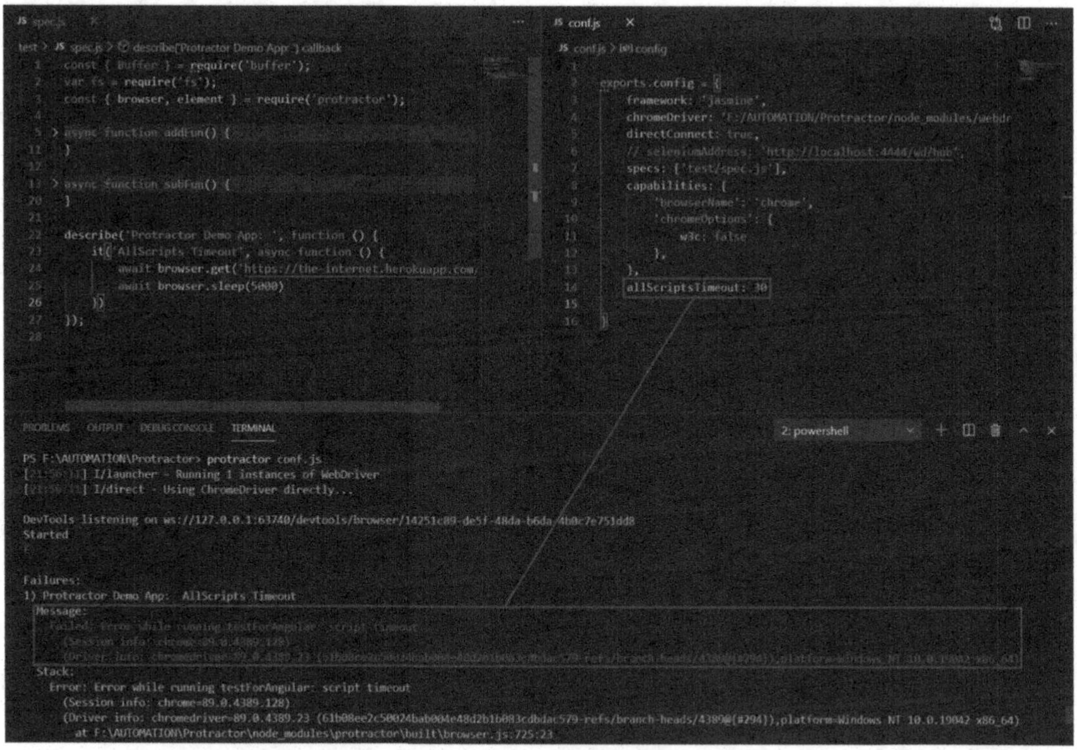

Figure 8-12. *Position of Jasmine default timeout in the test suite*

Timeouts: Jasmine Spec Timeout

The spec timeout defines the maximum time an it block can take to execute. It can be added to the conf.js file, as shown in Figure 8-13.

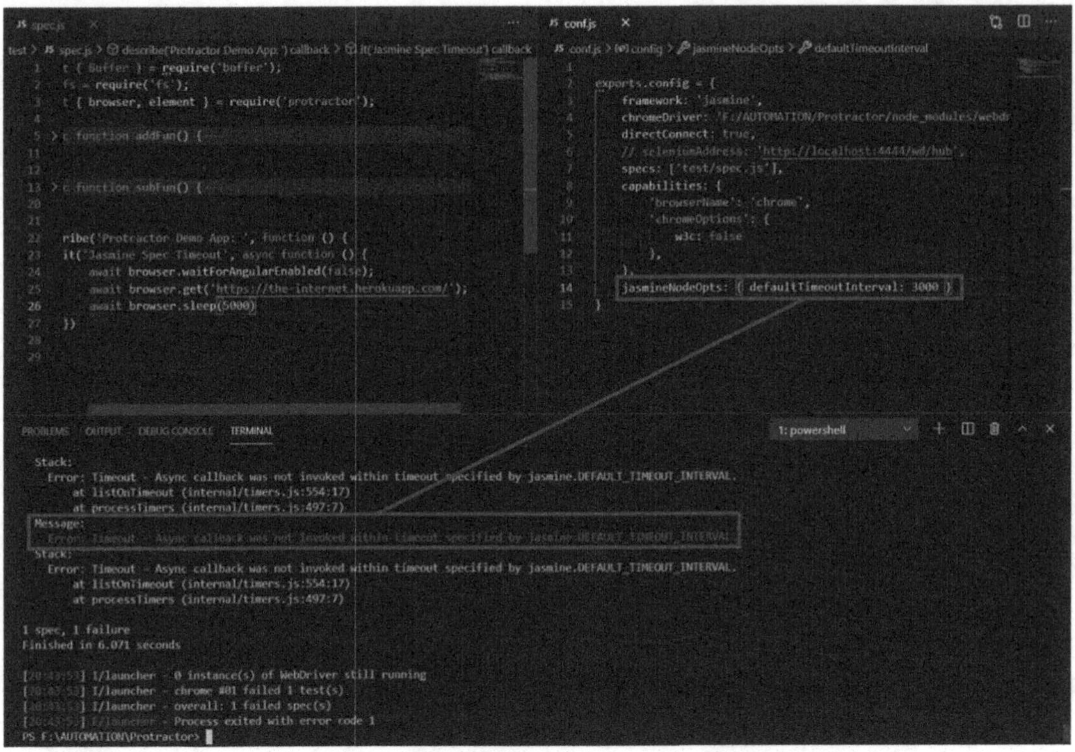

Figure 8-13. *Position of Jasmine default timeout in the test suite*

Timeouts: Selenium Server Start Timeout

You can use the `seleniumServerStartTimeout: 90000` option in your `conf.js` file. If Selenium jars take longer than usual to load and spin up the browser, it is required. The timeout is in milliseconds, and it waits for a local stand-alone Selenium server to start.

When the Selenium server takes longer than the specified time to start, you see the error shown in Figure 8-14.

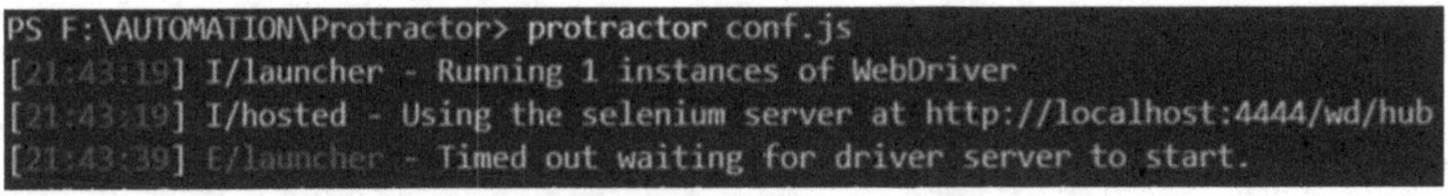

```
PS F:\AUTOMATION\Protractor> protractor conf.js
[21:43:19] I/launcher - Running 1 instances of WebDriver
[21:43:19] I/hosted - Using the selenium server at http://localhost:4444/wd/hub
[21:43:39] E/launcher - Timed out waiting for driver server to start.
```

Figure 8-14. *Selenium server startup timeout*

Summary

In this chapter, you saw different kinds of waits and timeouts. If you have a background in Selenium, you must have observed that an implicit wait is in the form of a timeout instead of a wait. Implicit waits are applied over the entirety of time the browser session is open, so it's an overall wait rather than element-specific. Hence it is better suited as a timeout.

The next chapter looks at framework design using Protractor.

CHAPTER 9

Framework Options and Design Pattern

In the last chapter, you saw waits and timeouts. Protractor can be used with different types of frameworks. Choosing a framework depends on a lot of different factors. Protractor's flexibility allows it to be implemented using any of the frameworks on the market. This chapter looks at the following, including frameworks that are compatible with Protractor.

- Framework introduction

- Protractor with TypeScript and Cucumber BDD

- Protractor with Jasmine

- Protractor with Mocha

- Protractor with Serenity/JavaScript

- Design patterns and introduction to the Page Object Model

Framework Introduction

A framework is an organized structure of code. It maintains the code to make a test project simpler and more efficient. This is done by breaking the code into smaller pieces or modules, which are logical and complete in their own perspective. Think of a house as a metaphor for framework. You don't build a house with only one room. You separate it according to the rooms' functionalities. The kitchen is used for cooking, and s bedroom is for sleeping. When you paint your kitchen, you don't want your bedroom impacted by the process. Similarly, a framework makes you aware of where changes need to be made and makes sure that the changes in one part of the framework don't impact the rest of it.

© Shashank Shukla 2021
S. Shukla, *The Protractor Handbook*, https://doi.org/10.1007/978-1-4842-7289-3_9

Protractor with TypeScript and Cucumber BDD

Although JavaScript is a great programming language, it is fundamentally a functional programming language and not an object-oriented one, at least before ES6 updates were available. It is also not a strongly typed, meaning many issues with the code are found during runtime instead of compile time. Hence, many programmers prefer TypeScript as their go-to language while using Protractor. TypeScript should not be confused with framework. It is a programming language and can be used with Mocha, Jasmine, or Serenity. TypeScript has the syntax similar to an object-oriented language and it can be compiled to JavaScript if required. TypeScript codes are easily maintainable, and developers are less likely to make syntactical mistakes because of its strongly typed feature. Another advantage is that TypeScript is created by Microsoft and has out-of-the-box support for IntelliSense in Visual Studio Code.

On the other hand, Cucumber is a behavior-driven development (BDD) framework. BDD is an Agile development process that encourages close collaboration between developers, testers, and business analysts during the product development lifecycle. This framework is used when testing high-level application behavior where business and product teams can closely monitor and contribute to writing tests instead of developing only unit tests.

Figure 9-1 shows the basic process of BDD. Cucumber is also compatible with other programming languages.

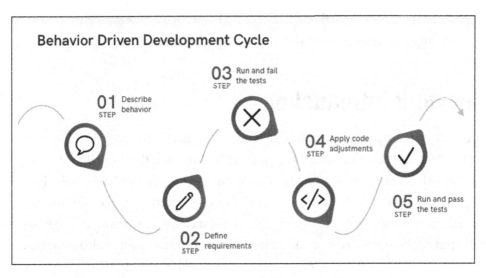

Figure 9-1. *BDD development cycle www.mobileappdaily.com/ behavior-driven-development*

The Cucumber framework is a boon, especially when your team closely collaborates with business analysts and product owners, because the BDD assertion style that Cucumber provides using Gherkin is very business-friendly.

Given steps describe the initial context of the system—the *scene* of the scenario. It is typically something that happened in the *past*.

When steps describe an event or an *action*, which could be a person interacting with the system or an event triggered by another system.

Then steps describe an *expected* outcome or result.

If you have successive a Given, When, or Then, you *could* use And, as shown in Listing 9-1.

Listing 9-1. Feature File Syntax

```
Scenario: User can search with "Google Search"
  Given I'm on the homepage
  When I type "Protractor" into the search field
  And I click the Google Search button
  Then I go to the Protractor home page from first search result
```

For more information, please visit the official Cucumber web site at `https://cucumber.io/docs/gherkin/reference/`.

You can also download the official boilerplate for integrating Protractor with Cucumber using TypeScript; see `https://github.com/wswebcreation/protractor-cucumber-typescript-boilerplate`.

Protractor with Jasmine

Jasmine is the framework used in this book so far. It was created in 2008. As the taglines in the official documentation say, it is "fast and has batteries included", meaning it provides testers with all the out-of-the-box features they need to test their software. You may recognize the familiar syntax in Listing 9-2.

Listing 9-2. Jasmine Way of Organizing the Tests

```
describe("A suite is just a function", function() {
  var a;
  it("and so is a spec", function() {
    a = true;
    expect(a).toBe(true);
  });
});
```

Protractor with Mocha

Mocha is a highly customizable framework. It doesn't aim to be a complete framework. Mocha provides developers a foundation and enables them to add their own custom extensions for assertions, code coverage, spies, fake data, reporting, and screenshots. This is why Chai is integrated; it is a popular assertion library. Listing 9-3 shows that the Mocha syntax and the Jasmine syntax are the same, and the first parameter provides a plain English description of the test case. The Jasmine framework has its own assertion library.

Listing 9-3. Mocha Way Of Organizing The Tests

```
describe("A suite is just a function", function() {
  var a;
  it("and so is a spec", function() {
    a = true;
    expect(a).toBe(true);
  });
});
```

Figure 9-2 compares three important frameworks that can be integrated with Protractor.

Figure 9-2. *Comparison of the frameworks provided by https://stackshare.io/*

Design Pattern Introduction

When designing a test framework, you must keep the test logic separated from the test data and the located web elements. A design pattern is a reusable solution for commonly occurring problems. For simplicity, you have only worked with one file (i.e., spec.js). Let's reuse an example from earlier chapters to automate a web app called OrangeHRM (see Figure 9-3).

Figure 9-3. *OrangeHRM Login page*

Look at Listing 9-4. You can label the pieces of code as different categories. The URL is constant, but part of it may change, depending on which part of the web site is being visited. It has locators like txtUsername, which is from the web page. It has test data, like Admin and admin123. It has functions that help users achieve actions, like sendKeys() and click(). It also has some generic or base functions, like sleep. And finally, it has the assertion necessary to verify the validation point. When looking at the code, you feel that it is clunky and hard to read.

Listing 9-4. Respective It Block of the Login Page of OrangeHRM Web Site

```
it('To validate the welcome message text of the landing page contains
"Welcome" string', async function () {
    await browser.waitForAngularEnabled(false);
    await browser.get('https://opensource-demo.orangehrmlive.com/');
    element(by.id('txtUsername')).sendKeys('Admin');
    element(by.id('txtPassword')).sendKeys('admin123');
    element(by.id('btnLogin')).click();
    browser.sleep(3000);
    var welcome_msg = element(by.id('welcome')).getText();
    expect(welcome_msg).toContain('Welcome');
})
```

Let's try to fix it using the Page Object Model (POM), a design pattern that is commonly used in Selenium for automating test cases. This design pattern can be used with a framework like keyword-driven, data-driven, and hybrid framework. POM directs that each web page in the application should have a corresponding page class, and the web page's elements should be the variables inside that class. The actions performed on the elements should be methods of the class. The naming conventions should be easy to read and related to the tasks they perform.

The first step in optimizing the code is to make a pageobjects folder and a base.js file inside it and a folder and a testdata.js file in the framework. Let's automate a landing page and a login page for the web app, and create their respective pages—landing.page.js and login.page.js.

The framework should look like Figure 9-4.

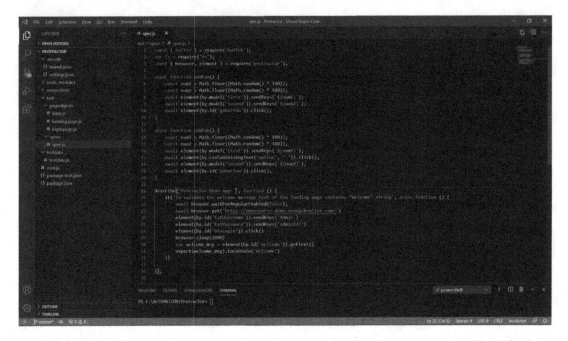

Figure 9-4. *Framework snapshot after creating all the necessary files and folders*

You are using ES6 features that are provided by JavaScript-like class keywords. ES6 is also known as ECMAScript 6 or ECMAScript 2015. It is a newer version of JavaScript with enhanced features.

Now let's look at the relevance of each file.

base.js

This file contains all the helper methods that are web-page agnostic, meaning the methods used across the web application. All the page files inherit this file, so the page files can access the generic methods of the web app. The URL is always constant in the app. It is good to separate it from the `spec.js` file and move it to the `base.js` file.

Let's create a class named `Base` inside `base.js`. A JavaScript class is syntactic sugar and doesn't correlate to a class in Java. A JavaScript class is a type of function behind the curtains.

Define a method inside the class named `openHomePage()`, where you mention the web page's base URL. Listing 9-5 has the contents of the `base.js` file. Export the contents of the `base.js` file with the `module.export` command, which is a Node.js feature available by default to organize and abstract the code. You import it later in the page file.

Listing 9-5. Contents of base.js File

```
module.exports = class Base {

    openHomePage(path) {
        return browser.url(`https://opensource-demo.orangehrmlive.
        com/${path}`)
    }

    pauseShort() {
        return browser.pause(3000)
    }

}
```

login.page.js

The login.page.js file has a LoginPage class that extends the Base class from the base.js file via the require keyword, meaning it inherits the base page's methods. The LoginPage class has locators, methods, and overridden parent class methods. Locators are defined using a Getter function, which has wider use, but in this context, using a getter provides simpler syntax by avoiding () when accessing the method.

Methods are all the actions performed on the page, like setValue and click. You override the parent methods to adapt to the page Class. The login.page.js file is shown in Listing 9-6.

Listing 9-6. Contents of login.page.js File

```
const Base = require('./base');

class LoginPage extends Base {

    get LoginInputBox() {
        return element(by.id('txtUsername'))
    }

    get PasswordInputBox() {
        return element(by.id('txtPassword'))
    }
```

```
    get LoginButton() {
        return element(by.id('btnLogin'))
    }

    fillUsername() {
        return this.LoginInputBox.sendKeys("Admin")
    }

    fillPassword() {
        return this.PasswordInputBox.sendKeys("admin123")
    }

    clickLoginButton() {
        return this.LoginButton.click()
    }

    openHomePage() {
        return super.openHomePage('')
    }
}

module.exports = new LoginPage()
```

landing.page.js

Some part of the end-to-end test case in Listing 9-4 spills over to the web app's landing page after the login step, where you eventually validate the Welcome message, as highlighted in Figure 9-5.

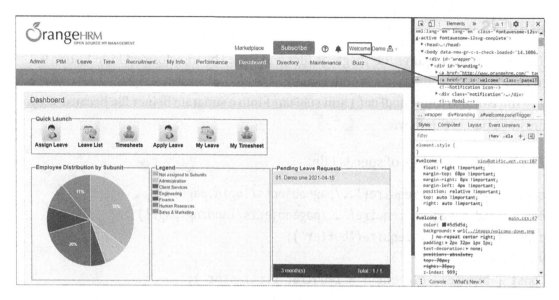

Figure 9-5. *Landing page logo attribute verification*

You need to capture the elements of this landing page in a new page object file named landing.page.js. This file also requires a base.js file, and it has the LandingPage class. The class uses the <a> tag's element locator strategy and a function that makes the assertion. The function is not hard-coded, so the parameters are provided by the user from the spec.js file to maintain flexibility. Lastly, this file is exported like login.page.js, so it is required in spec.js. The contents of this file are shown in Listing 9-7.

Listing 9-7. Contents of landing.page.js File

```
const Base = require('./base');

class LandingPage extends Base {

    get welcome_msg() {
        return element(by.id('welcome'))
    }

    verifyTextContaining(text) {
        expect(this.welcome_msg.getText()).toContain(text)
    }

}

module.exports = new LandingPage();
```

spec.js

The spec.js file requires the .page.js files and hence be transformed from Listing 9-4 to Listing 9-8. The difference is noticeable.

You can also throw addFun() and subFun() into a separate helper file because they are not a part of this flow.

Listing 9-8. Contents of spec.js File

```
const LoginPage = require('../pageobjects/login.page')
const LandingPage = require('../pageobjects/landing.page')
const { Buffer } = require('buffer');
var fs = require('fs');
const { browser, element } = require('protractor');

describe('Protractor Demo App: ', function () {
    it('To validate the welcome message text of the landing page contains
    "Welcome" string', async function () {
        await browser.waitForAngularEnabled(false);
        LoginPage.openHomePage();
        LoginPage.fillUsername();
        LoginPage.fillPassword();
        LoginPage.clickLoginButton();
        LandingPage.pauseShort();
        LandingPage.verifyTextContaining('Welcome');
    })

});
```

EXERCISE

There is a lot of room for improvement and optimization in the framework. I would like you to integrate the following functionalities into their respective files in the framework.

1. Add a screenshot helper function.

2. Add waitForAngular to a helper function named Angular(off).

3. Add a 10-second pause named longPause().

4. Abstract the test data, 'admin' and 'admin123', to its own separate file named testdata.js.

5. Add a new function for asserting the height and width of the logo element.

6. Add a "Forgot password" user journey (the base URL needs to be appended to the forgot password link).

Summary

Protractor is extremely flexible and can be customized to work with different frameworks. Figure 9-6 provides a high-level comparison of the frameworks.

Features	Protractor with			
	Mocha	Jasmine	Typescript	Cucumber
Programming language	JavaScript	JavaScript	Typescript	JavaScript
Category	Unit Testing, Intergration Testing, End-to-End	Unit Testing, Intergration Testing, End-to-End Testing	Unit Testing, Intergration Testing, End-to-End Testing	Acceptance Testing
General info	Simple, flexible, fun javascript test framework for node.js & the browser	DOM-less simple JavaScript testing framework. Jasmine is a "batteries included" Behavior Driven Development testing framework for JavaScript	TypeScript extends JavaScript programming language by adding types. Types provide a way to describe the shape of an object, providing better documentation, and allowing TypeScript to validate that your code is working correctly.	Cucumber is a software tool that supports behavior-driven development.
Licence	Open Source	Open Source	Open Source	Open Source with Pro option
Framework Type	Hybrid	Hybrid	Hybrid	Hybrid
Assertions	Not available	Built in	Not available	Built in
Promise Support	Available	Available	Available	Available

Figure 9-6. *Protractor integrated with different frameworks*

This chapter discussed the frameworks that are compatible with Protractor. It also discussed the Page Object Model design pattern used to organize a test suite.

The next chapter looks at a Protractor configuration file and how to customize it.

CHAPTER 10

Configuration File

So far in the automation journey, you have interacted with conf.js files in a very limited capacity. Now that you can smoothly design and execute the test cases in Protractor, and you understand the basics of framework design, it is time to familiarize yourself with some of the configuration settings offered by the Protractor tool. All configurations are listed in the conf.js file. Let's go through some of these settings and their relevance in some major functions, like reporting and parallel execution.

This chapter covers some of the following configuration settings in the conf.js file.

- Direct connect

- Path to test files via specs

- How to exclude files via exclude

- logLevel

- Reporting

  - Reporter

- Parallel execution

  - Capabilities

  - Max instances

Direct Connect

Protractor provides a facility to turn off WebDriver binary files and can connect to Chrome and Firefox browsers directly. Figure 10-1 shows the setting in the config. js file, where you have turned off or commented the Selenium address and added directConnect: true and the optional chromeDriver path.

© Shashank Shukla 2021
S. Shukla, *The Protractor Handbook*, https://doi.org/10.1007/978-1-4842-7289-3_10

```
JS conf.js > [@] config
 1
 2    exports.config = {
 3        framework: 'jasmine',
 4        chromeDriver: 'F:/AUTOMATION/Protractor/node_modules/webdriver-manager/selenium/chromedriver.exe',
 5        directConnect: true,
 6        // seleniumAddress: 'http://localhost:4444/wd/hub',
 7        specs: ['test/specs/spec.js'],
 8        capabilities: {
 9            'browserName': 'chrome',
10            'chromeOptions': {
11                w3c: false
12            },
13        },
14        allScriptsTimeout: 30
15
16    }
```

Figure 10-1. *directConnect configuration setting*

Using a Selenium address offers you access to the test script logs, which is not provided by the directConnect option. Figure 10-2 shows the console terminal message that lets the user know the test is being run by the directConnect option.

```
PS F:\AUTOMATION\Protractor> protractor conf.js
[11:59:24] I/launcher - Running 1 instances of WebDriver
[11:59:24] I/direct - Using ChromeDriver directly...

DevTools listening on ws://127.0.0.1:61443/devtools/browser/7a7b1d2b-5e4
Started
.


1 spec, 0 failures
Finished in 4.383 seconds

[11:59:30] I/launcher - 0 instance(s) of WebDriver still running
[11:59:30] I/launcher - chrome #01 passed
PS F:\AUTOMATION\Protractor>
```

Figure 10-2. *directConnect log in console terminal*

Specs

The specs parameter tells Protractor where the test files are located. The value in Figure 10-3 tells Protractor to look out for a file named speck.js in the specs folder, which is available in the test folder located in the root directory.

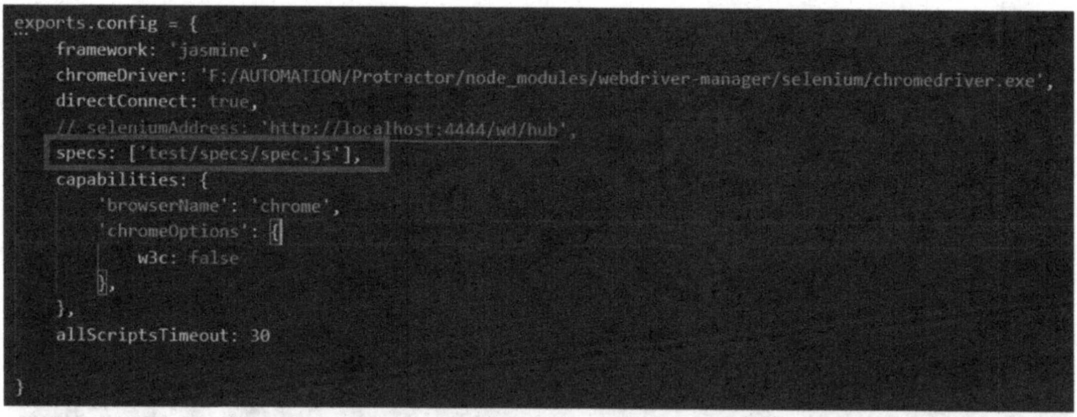

```
exports.config = {
    framework: 'jasmine',
    chromeDriver: 'F:/AUTOMATION/Protractor/node_modules/webdriver-manager/selenium/chromedriver.exe',
    directConnect: true,
    // seleniumAddress: 'http://localhost:4444/wd/hub',
    specs: ['test/specs/spec.js'],
    capabilities: {
        'browserName': 'chrome',
        'chromeOptions': {
            w3c: false
        },
    },
    allScriptsTimeout: 30
}
```

Figure 10-3. *Config file specs parameter*

Exclude

The exclude parameter prohibits the test runner from picking up a file in its value.
Figure 10-4 shows that the backup.js file is mentioned in the exclude parameter, so only
spec.js is displayed in the results.

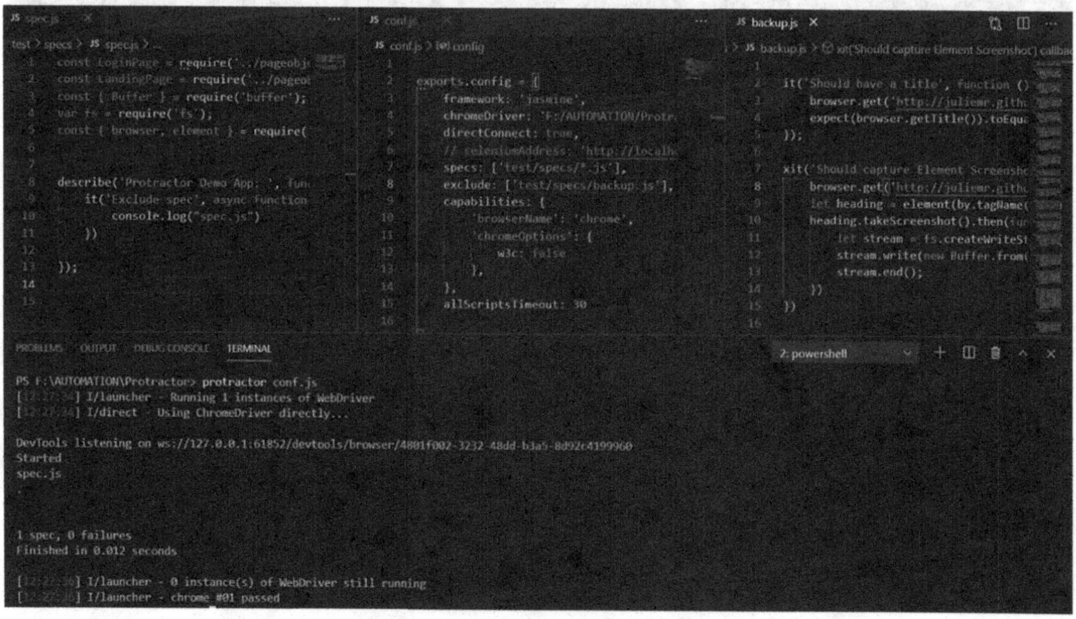

Figure 10-4. *backup.js file excluded in the run*

Suites

You can segregate your spec files into various suites, like Smoke and Regression. As shown in Figure 10-5, you can run different specs inside the suite per requirements. A single spec can be a part of multiple suites.

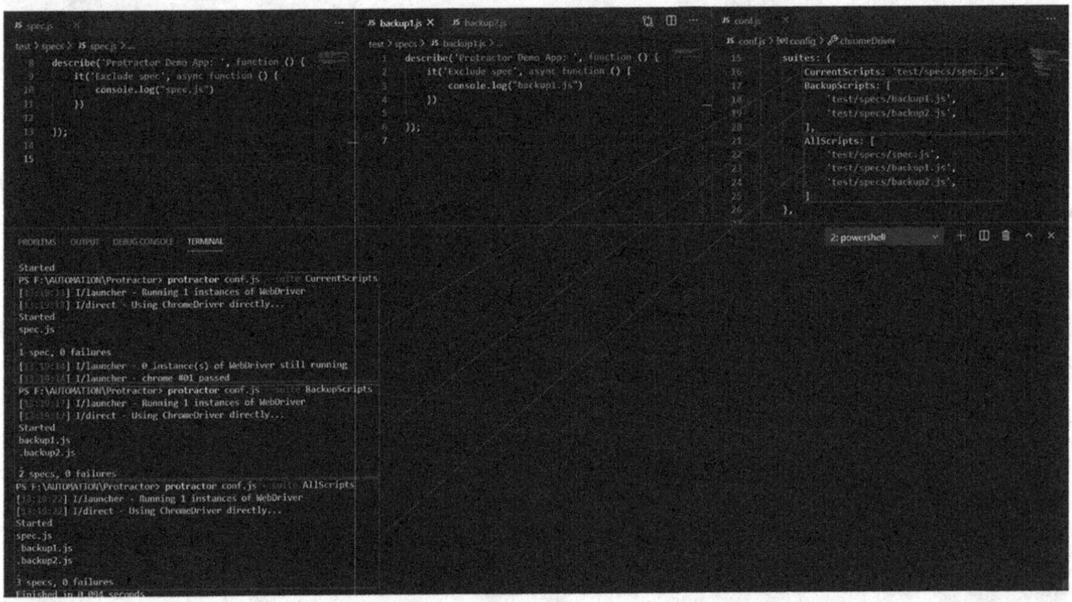

Figure 10-5. *Suites running in Protractor*

Hooks

With hooks, you can execute custom functions at any point in time during a test life cycle in Protractor. Some hooks are provided by Protractor, and some are provided by Jasmine. For instance, there are times when you want to maximize the browser before each test script. This can be done using the beforeEach hook provided by Jasmine. Similarly, beforeAll and afterAll are run before executing the first it block and after executing the last it block, respectively.

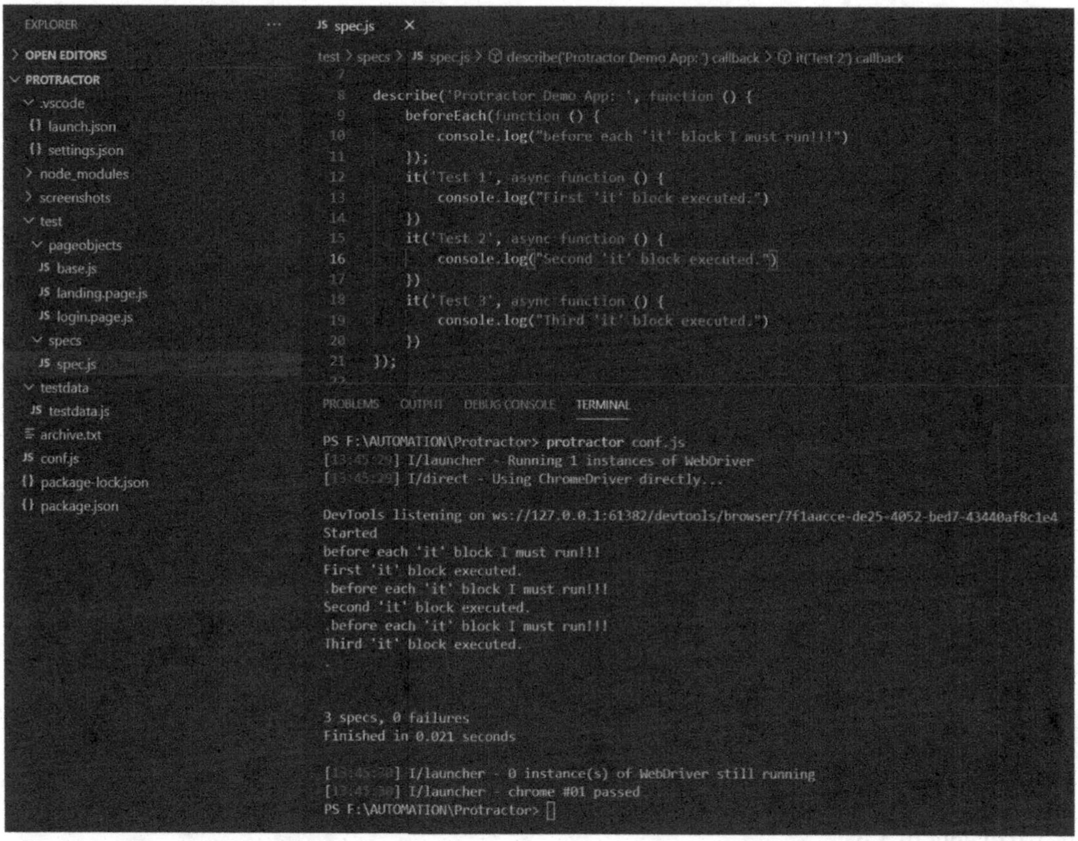

Figure 10-6. *beforeEach hook*

There are other hooks that can be set up directly in the conf.js file. They are called *lifecycle hooks*. The beforeLaunch(), onPrepare(), onComplete(), onCleanup(), and afterLaunch() hooks fall into this category. The following are some of the hooks that are commonly used when working with Protractor and the Jasmine framework.

```
--- beforeLaunch
    --- onPrepare
        --- beforeAll
            --- beforeEach
            +++ afterEach
        +++ afterAll
    +++ onComplete
+++ afterLaunch
```

Figure 10-7 shows lifecycle hooks that can be set up directly using the conf.js file.

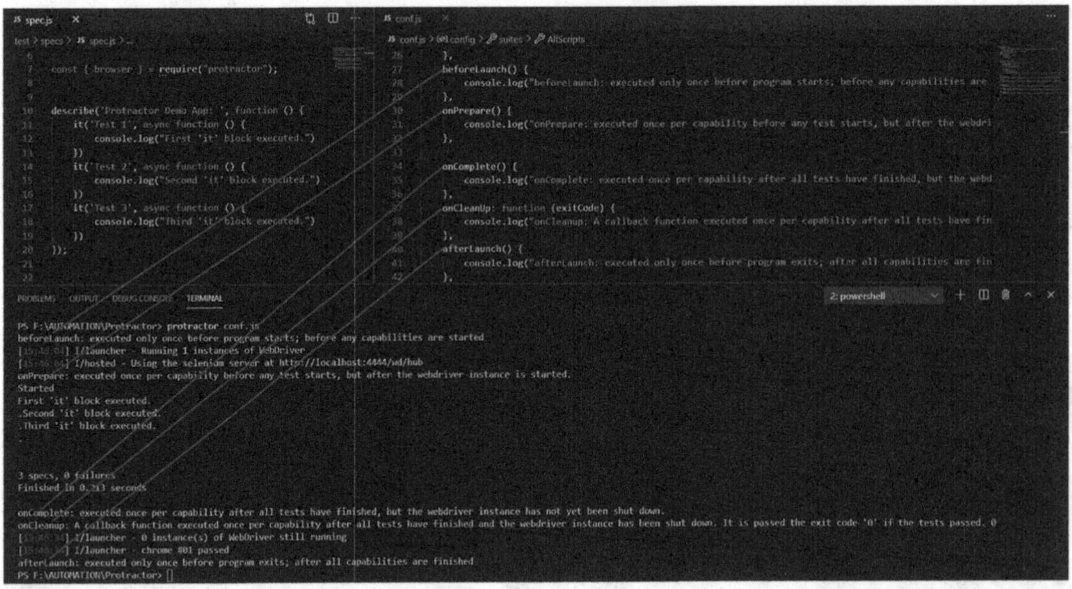

Figure 10-7. *Different hooks populating at different times of the execution*

The conf.js code for the hooks is shown in Listing 10-1.

Listing 10-1. Lifecycle Hooks in conf.js File

```
beforeLaunch() {
    console.log("beforeLaunch: executed only once before program starts;
    before any capabilities are started")
},
onPrepare() {
    console.log("onPrepare: executed once per capability before any test
    starts, but after the webdriver instance is started.")
},

onComplete() {
    console.log("onComplete: executed once per capability after all tests
    have finished, but the webdriver instance has not yet been shut down.")
},
```

```
onCleanUp: function (exitCode) {
    console.log("onCleanup: A callback function executed once per
    capability after all tests have finished and the webdriver instance has
    been shut down. It is passed the exit code '0' if the tests passed. " +
    exitCode);
},
afterLaunch() {
    console.log("afterLaunch: executed only once before program exits;
    after all capabilities are finished")
},
```

Reporters

Protractor provides integration with different reporters. protractor-beautiful-reporter is a reporter that can integrate with Protractor and create some of the most visually appealing reports after execution.

To install the reporter, run npm install protractor-beautiful-reporter --save-dev in the console terminal. Once the reporter is successfully installed, you should see the message shown in Figure 10-8 in your terminal.

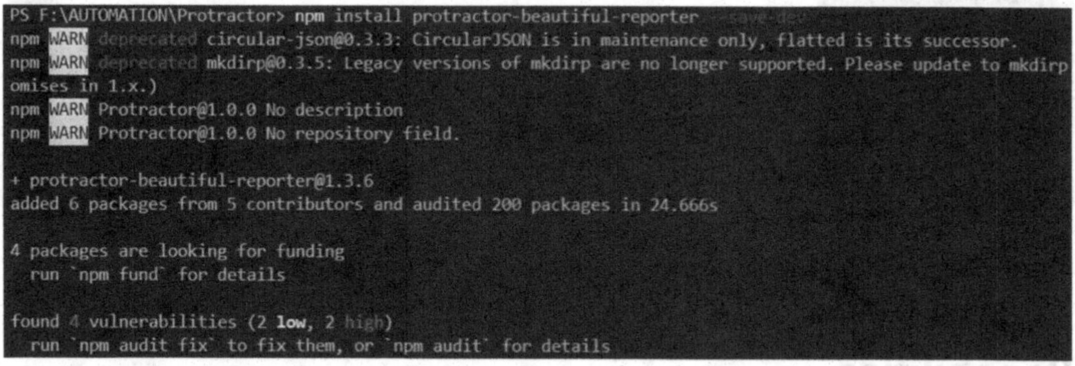

Figure 10-8. protractor-beautiful-reporter install successful

Now replace the code inside the onPrepare hook in the last example with the code in Listing 10-2.

Listing 10-2. Adding Reporter to onPrepare Hook

```
onPrepare: function () {
    jasmine.getEnv().addReporter(new HtmlReporter({
        baseDirectory: 'reports'
    }).getJasmine2Reporter());
},
```

As you start the execution, you see a folder generated in the framework. And when you open `report.html` inside the folder in Chrome or any other browser, you find a beautiful report marking the status of the last execution, as shown in Figure 10-9.

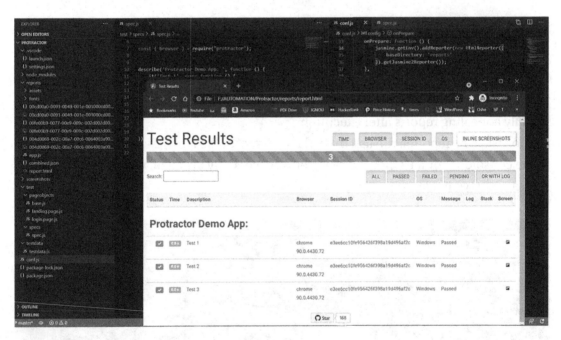

Figure 10-9. *Report in Chrome browser*

Capabilities

By default, the test cases are run sequentially one at a time by Protractor. But there are situations where you need the test cases to run in parallel, such as when doing multi-browser testing or when there are thousands of cases as part of a regression suite that must run continually in a CI process. You can do it with the help of `capabilities` parameters in the `conf.js` configuration file.

Look at the configuration file settings to run Protractor test cases in parallel. Before starting the parallel execution, there are few steps that you must follow.

First, remove the .js extension from the current spec file that you are working on so that Protractor doesn't pick it up for execution. Next, create a new spec file with the content provided in Listing 10-3 and make nine more replicas of that spec file, as shown in Figure 10-10.

Listing 10-3. Simple Test Case for Parallel Execution

```
var path = require('path');
var currentFileName = path.basename(__filename);
describe('Protractor Demo App: ', function () {
    it('Parallel Testing file:-', async function () {
        await browser.get('http://juliemr.github.io/protractor-demo/');
        console.log("Executed File- " + currentFileName);
    })
})
```

Figure 10-10. *The framework should look like this*

Now that you have ten spec files, go to the conf.js file and find parameters called shardTestFiles and maxInstances. They should be set similar to the conf.js file's content, as shown in Listing 10-4.

Listing 10-4. conf.js file Content

```
var HtmlReporter = require('protractor-beautiful-reporter');

exports.config = {
    framework: 'jasmine',
    seleniumAddress: 'http://localhost:4444/wd/hub',
    specs: ['test/specs/*.js'],
    capabilities: {
        'browserName': 'chrome',
        shardTestFiles: true,
        maxInstances: 5,
        'chromeOptions': {
            w3c: false
        },
    },
    onPrepare: function () {
        jasmine.getEnv().addReporter(new HtmlReporter({
            baseDirectory: 'reports'
        }).getJasmine2Reporter());
    },
}
```

Let's look at these options before starting parallel execution. The maxInstance parameter inside the capabilities parameter is the number of browser instances that Protractor can spawn during execution. And when the ShardTestFiles parameter is set to true, it enables the sharing of tests at the spec level, which achieves parallel testing.

Run the tests, and you notice five browser instances pop up and execute the ten spec files within seconds.

Figure 10-11 shows the results of the run. Ensure the report folder is deleted before a fresh run.

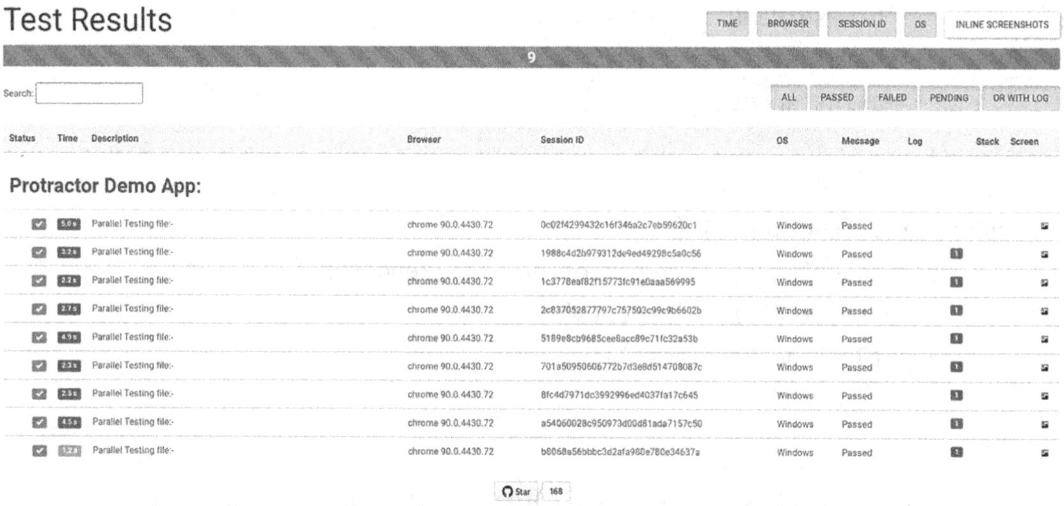

Test Results

Figure 10-11. *Parallel run report*

Now let's take another browser into account. If you have one spec file and two capabilities (i.e., Chrome and Firefox) with maximum instances of 7 and 3, respectively, the same spec file runs in Chrome and Firefox in parallel. maxSessions: 10 caps the number of browsers that can be spawned by Protractor during execution, which is ten in this case. The configuration is shown in Listing 10-5.

Listing 10-5. conf.js File Content for Multi-Browser Testing

```
var HtmlReporter = require('protractor-beautiful-reporter');

exports.config = {
    framework: 'jasmine',
    seleniumAddress: 'http://localhost:4444/wd/hub',
    specs: ['test/specs/*.js'],
    maxSessions: 10,
    multiCapabilities: [
        {
            'browserName': 'chrome',
            shardTestFiles: true,
            maxInstances: 7,

        },
        {
```

```
            'browserName': 'firefox',
            shardTestFiles: true,
            maxInstances: 3,
        },
    ],
    onPrepare: function () {
        jasmine.getEnv().addReporter(new HtmlReporter({
            baseDirectory: 'reports'
        }).getJasmine2Reporter());
    },
}
```

This results in each spec file are run in Chrome and Firefox in parallel (a maximum of seven instances in Chrome and three instances in Firefox). You see seven Chrome and three Firefox browsers spawning at any given time. The report provides more insight into the tested specs and their performance, as shown in Figure 10-12.

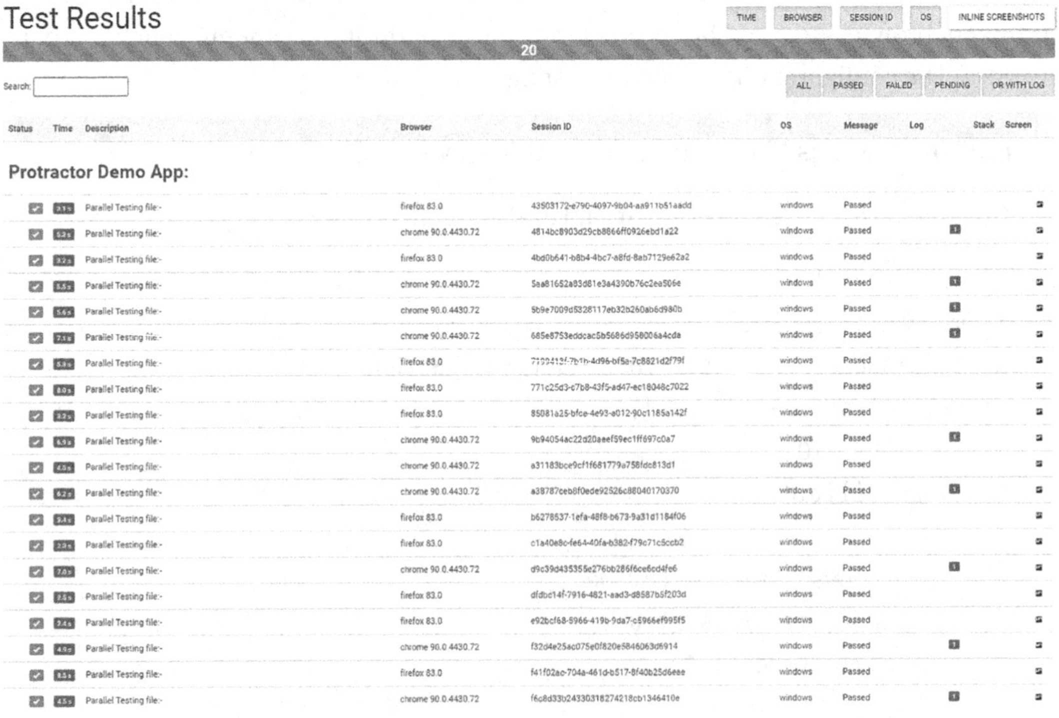

Figure 10-12. *Ten spec files distributed among two browsers running parallelly. Total specs run are 20*

You see in the console log that the spec files were distributed between the two browsers, and at any given time, no more than five instances of each browser were open, as shown in Figure 10-13.

```
[22:15:08] I/testLogger -

[22:15:08] I/launcher - 0 instance(s) of WebDriver still running
[22:15:08] I/launcher - chrome #01-1 passed
[22:15:08] I/launcher - chrome #01-0 passed
[22:15:08] I/launcher - chrome #01-5 passed
[22:15:08] I/launcher - chrome #01-4 passed
[22:15:08] I/launcher - chrome #01-3 passed
[22:15:08] I/launcher - chrome #01-2 passed
[22:15:08] I/launcher - chrome #01-6 passed
[22:15:08] I/launcher - chrome #01-8 passed
[22:15:08] I/launcher - chrome #01-9 passed
[22:15:08] I/launcher - chrome #01-7 passed
[22:15:08] I/launcher - firefox #11-1 passed
[22:15:08] I/launcher - firefox #11-3 passed
[22:15:08] I/launcher - firefox #11-0 passed
[22:15:08] I/launcher - firefox #11-2 passed
[22:15:08] I/launcher - firefox #11-6 passed
[22:15:08] I/launcher - firefox #11-4 passed
[22:15:08] I/launcher - firefox #11-7 passed
[22:15:08] I/launcher - firefox #11-8 passed
[22:15:08] I/launcher - firefox #11-9 passed
[22:15:08] I/launcher - firefox #11-5 passed
PS F:\AUTOMATION\Protractor>
```

Figure 10-13. *Console message logging the spawning of the two browsers and their browser instances*

Summary

In this chapter, you saw Protractor file configurations settings and learned how to use them to make flexible and feature-rich automation test cases. You also saw how the reporter and parallel testing work and learned the relevance of configuration files.

Let's sum up the Protractor automation journey by looking at some of the pros and cons of the tool in the next chapter.

CHAPTER 11

Conclusion

This chapter concludes the book's Protractor test automation journey. You started the journey by setting up the Protractor test tool, learning how to install the framework and its related dependencies, and running a demo spec file. This was followed by a discussion on the methods to locate Angular elements using selector strategies provided by Selenium and Protractor. Then you learned about the Protractor APIs that automate various user actions on located elements.

You also learned some of Protractor's useful assertion methods along with some Jasmine assertions. Chapter 8 discussed the importance of waits in automation testing and implemented various wait commands provided by the tool. In the same chapter, you learned about timeouts, which are very important in ensuring the robustness of test cases and the test suite in general. Next, the various framework options provided by Protractor were discussed, and you learned about the Page Object Model design pattern. Finally, you learned Protractor configuration settings and how to integrate the reporter and execute tests in parallel with configuration file changes. The examples covered in this book leave you well-equipped to explore the countless possibilities of Protractor and Node.js-based automation testing.

As this book wraps up, let's discuss some of the advantages, disadvantages, and challenges associated with the tool.

© Shashank Shukla 2021
S. Shukla, *The Protractor Handbook*, https://doi.org/10.1007/978-1-4842-7289-3_11

The Advantages of Using Protractor

- Setting up and installing the framework is simple for non-programmers, as you saw in Chapter 1.

- It runs on Selenium WebDriver, which means that all Selenium features are inherited by this tool. As mentioned in Chapter 1, it is a JavaScript/Node.js implementation of the Selenium WebDriver API, and hence you also get the power and flexibility of Selenium in your tests. You can verify this in the Dependencies section at `www.npmjs.com/package/protractor`, as shown in Figure 11-1.

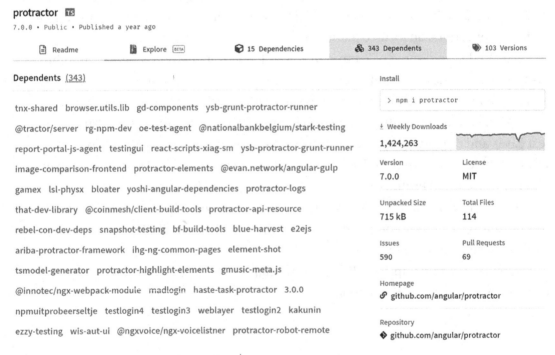

Figure 11-1. *Protractor dependencies*

- It has good support to identify Angular-specific elements, as shown in Chapters 2 and 3.

- It offers synchronous implementation of asynchronous browser commands. As you might have noticed, complex JavaScript features like promises to control the execution flow were not used in this book. `async/await` ensures the statements are executed sequentially. It results in simpler syntax than Selenium WebDriverJS, which is vanilla WebDriverJS and most other frameworks, as you saw in Chapters 4, 5, and 6 when using browser API methods.

- Waits and timeouts in Protractor are handled in a more effective manner with easy-to-understand syntax, as you saw in Chapter 8.

- Protractor is highly flexible, letting you choose your favorite testing framework (Jasmine, Mocha, Cucumber) and design pattern, as discussed in Chapter 9.

- Parallel execution is easy to set up with the help of a simplified `conf.js` file, as demonstrated in Chapter 10.

The Disadvantages of Using Protractor

- Protractor's API documentation can be overwhelming for beginners or people switching from Java-based test automation tools.

- It only supports JavaScript, limiting the options for you and your team based on your programming language skills.

- The Selenium server needs to be started separately using a Selenium stand-alone npm utility. It is not managed by the framework itself.

- Robot Class, Sikuli, and AutoIT—tools that help with automating Windows-based applications—cannot be integrated into Protractor, so Windows application-based testing is not possible with it or any other tool based on Selenium WebDriver.

- Since it is an open source tool, it has known open issues (see `https://github.com/angular/protractor/issues`).

Challenges Faced When Using Protractor

- It is sometimes hard to trace errors in Protractor when a test fails, as you have noticed in your automation journey.

- The installation process covered in Chapter 1 can be a challenge if there are version compatibility issues between Chrome, Node. js, external libraries, and Protractor. It is always recommended to install the latest stable version of Protractor along with other external libraries or install the versions that are known to be compatible with each other.

- It does not have rich community support if there are any issues.

This book doesn't intend to cover every aspect associated with the Protractor automation tool. Instead, it acts as a go-to API reference guide for people whose main interest is to explore this tool hands-on and go beyond basic knowledge. Much of your Protractor and automation testing proficiency will come from practice and experience. As you gain experience, you will make better and more informed decisions on locator strategy selections, applying correct waits, and using meaningful assertions.

I wish you good luck in your future automation journey with Protractor and other evolving Node.js-based automation tools.

Index

© Shashank Shukla 2021
S. Shukla, *The Protractor Handbook*, https://doi.org/10.1007/978-1-4842-7289-3